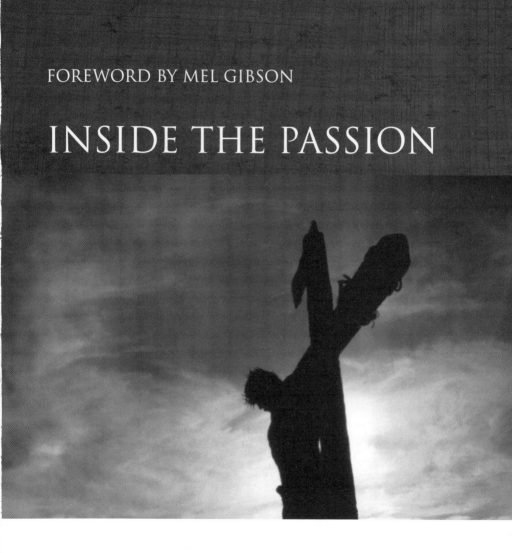

FOREWORD BY MEL GIBSON

INSIDE THE PASSION

AN INSIDER'S LOOK AT THE PASSION OF THE CHRIST

JOHN BARTUNEK, L.C.

Creative Director: Jim Bolton
Designed by: Rule29 Creative | www.rule29.com
Edited by: Bonne Steffen

Biblical text taken from the Douay-Rheims American Edition, 1899.

This edition distributed under publishing license from Dearborn Media Group, Inc. by:
Ascension Press
PO Box 1990
West Chester, PA 19380
www.ascensionpress.com
Orders: 800-376-0520

Published in the United States of America

ISBN: 1-932645-77-2

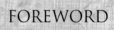
FOREWORD

Since the release of *The Passion of The Christ*, more people than I can count have told me they were moved by the film to open their Bibles and read or re-read the Gospels, especially the parts about Christ's suffering, death, and resurrection. They have been provoked to reflect on their own lives and their relationship with God. They are looking for answers to the many questions triggered by seeing the film.

This book by my friend Fr. John Bartunek provides a resource for people who want to know more—both about the meaning of the film and especially about its biblical and theological backdrop. As a man of faith and a scholar, Father John carefully examines a number of issues that simmer just beneath the surface of the film—vital issues like forgiveness, love, freedom, the role of Mary, salvation, and the meaning of suffering, human and divine. The time he spent with myself and others involved in the production gives him a unique and, I think, interesting perspective.

When I first decided to make this film I had little idea of what I was getting myself into. I just knew I had to make it. I wanted to help people understand and experience the suffering of Christ. Many audience members were moved to tears, but some were just mystified, and they still don't understand why the film has had an impact. I think the way audiences have reacted indicates a widespread thirst for the straight truth about God and man, and about what God was willing to go through to win us back to Himself. I hope this book helps people understand these truths in a deeper and fuller way.

Mel Gibson

INTRODUCTION

THE PHENOMENON

What makes a movie successful? You can call a movie successful simply based on box office returns, whether or not its story is edifying or its artistry meritorious. By box office standards, Mel Gibson's *The Passion of The Christ* was a soaring success. It ranks in the top ten movies for all time in the following categories: domestic opening day gross—ninth ($26.6 million, representing about 3.8 million viewers), domestic opening Wednesday gross—third, domestic weekend opening gross—sixth ($83.8 million, about 11 million viewers), domestic four-day opening gross—fourth ($97.3 million, almost 14 million viewers), domestic five-day opening gross—third ($125.2 million, almost 17 million viewers).

But the movie wasn't just a flash in the pan during the opening day releases. *The Passion of The Christ* ranks in the top 25 for all-time box office returns ($609 million, about 121 million viewers). When it was released on DVD and VHS, 9 million copies were sold in the first week—making it the top-selling live action title of all time for home entertainment.[1]

These impressive statistics are even more intriguing because the film is R-rated, is low-budget, religious in its scope, and uses two dead languages (Latin and Aramaic) rather than English. It doesn't even have a signature song that you can hum on your way out of the theater.

But none of these factors deterred moviegoers. People saw it. They saw it again with a friend. When the movie was available in a DVD/VHS format, they snatched up a copy. The audiences weren't solely religious people. During the movie's run, there were stories of murderers and other criminals who, after seeing the film, later surrendered to the police. The phenomenon left sociologists and market analysts scratching their heads.

It also left moviegoers scratching their heads—not about the phenomenon, but about the film itself. People wanted to talk about the movie. In the wake of its release, some churches even had higher turnouts for *Passion* discussion groups than for Sunday services.

1 www.zenit.org, September 9, 2004.

THE RESPONSE

The buzz had started months before the film opened in theaters. Private screenings of an initial version left audiences moved and wanting to know more. While Mel and company were looping and editing in Rome, I attended one of these screenings. (I had become involved in the film while they were still shooting in Rome where I was studying theology. I spent countless hours watching the filming and interacting with the actors and director.) The interest stirred up by that screening became the catalyst for this book.

My colleagues and I were deeply enriched by the film. As Catholic priests and seminarians, we had the advantage of familiarity with Christ's Passion recounted in the Bible. Yet we wondered, *Would most moviegoers appreciate the movie's unprecedented spiritual and religious significance, let alone its artistry?* Having spent time on the set with Mel Gibson, Jim Caviezel (who portrays Jesus), and other key players on the *Passion* team, I heard firsthand their personal motivations and the reasons behind their artistic choices. The average viewer didn't have those insights going into the theater, yet people were profoundly affected by the power of the *Passion's* message without understanding why. They wanted to know more.

It's not unlike a first-time tourist to Rome visiting St. Peter's Basilica, the largest and most ornate Christian church in the world. The beauty, immensity, and grandeur of the Basilica deeply impress every visitor, Catholic or not, whether or not they know the historical and artistic background of the building. The experience is real and emotional. But when the tour guide explains the meaning behind the art—why the building is there; what it signifies; why the statues and mosaics are arranged the way they are; who is depicted in the various works of art—the experience takes on a different perspective. Knowing the artists' intentions and the cultural-religious context that influenced them, an emotionally stirring trip to St. Peter's can easily become a life-changing milestone.

THE TASK

With that in mind, we proposed a book idea to Mel—a movie guidebook to enrich the typical "tourist" experiencing *The Passion of The Christ*. Originally, we envisioned the book as an extended interview, weaving Mel's own comments into an explanation of the historical and theological context of the

Christ's suffering. I left Rome to spend time with Mel and his post-production team in Los Angeles during the last few months before the film's release. For weeks I accompanied Mel, watching him work with the editors, the composer, the promotions team, and the press. I sat in on many of the private screenings organized by the movie companies, Icon and New Market, taking notes during the post-screening question-and-answer sessions. I spent hours alone with Mel, asking him questions about the film that no one else asked. He revealed the reasons behind some of the innumerable artistic choices that he was forced to make, choices that turned this small art-house project into an international blockbuster.

In the end, we agreed on this "inside look" approach to the book. We feared that an interview version would stifle discussion instead of stimulating it. Mel hopes that people will think and talk about the film, and he doesn't want his own words to be taken as the unique, official interpretation. After all, he didn't write a book about the Passion; he made a movie. That's how he communicates best, through the artistry of film. And just like any great work of art, this film transcends mere explanations, even those of the artist himself. But like St. Peter's Basilica, a few, well-chosen explanations of the context and the artist's intent can turn a passing, emotionally stimulating aesthetic experience into a deeply enriching spiritual encounter. With that in mind, let's take a look inside *The Passion*.

PART I: THE FIRST CONDEMNATION

—⊱✠⊰—

CHAPTER 1

COMBAT IN THE GARDEN

THE FIRST GLIMPSE OF JESUS

The film opens in an olive garden bathed in phosphorescent moonlight. The scene was filmed on a set in Cinecittà, Italy (with about twenty full grown olive trees temporarily transplanted into the studio), but it represents the Garden of Gethsemane, a real place that you can still visit today in Israel. Just east of the walls surrounding old Jerusalem, it takes about twenty minutes to walk to the Garden from the hall where Jesus and His twelve closest followers, the Apostles, had eaten their last Passover Seder together. The Gospels indicate that Jesus and the Apostles knew Gethsemane well and often passed their nights there, praying and sleeping. It is a famous garden, familiar to every Christian as the fated place where the Passion of Christ began.

The first sequence in the film tantalizes the audience by showing Jesus (portrayed by actor Jim Caviezel) from behind, in "dappled moonlight" (as noted in the screenplay). Viewers are disconcerted because Jesus' features are indiscernible. Everyone already has a mental picture of Jesus.

Subconsciously, viewers are all wondering if this Jesus will measure up. The camera doesn't let you see Christ's face at first, just his back, enveloped in the shadows. Preconceptions are pushed into the background; a fresh experience is about to unfold.

CHRIST IN AGONY

Christ's prayer in Gethsemane on the eve of His Passion is one of the most mysterious events recorded in the Gospels. Christians have meditated and reflected on it for centuries, but its spiritual richness is inexhaustible.

The word *Gethsemane* literally means "olive press," the place where harvested olives are crushed to extract their oil, one of the most widely used and significant commodities in the ancient world. In the Garden of Gethsemane, Christ too was crushed, by a spiritual and emotional crisis. The Gospels describe this excruciating moment as "being sorrowful unto death … being in agony …"[2] So horrendous was His moral suffering that "his sweat became as drops of blood, trickling down upon the ground."[3] Modern medicine confirms this description as an instance of intense human psychological stress so severe that capillaries near the surface of the skin burst, mixing blood with the sweat of anxiety. Nowhere else in the Gospels does Jesus even come close to a similar state of debility and confusion; at no other time does He ask His Apostles to stay awake and pray with Him, as if He is running out of strength.

The film captures this paradox in a striking contrast: Jesus' strong and virile physical presence with His agonizing, almost helpless emotional state, evident in the desperation characterizing His prayer. That contrast, intro-

2 Matthew 26:38, Mark 14:34, Luke 22:43.

3 Luke 22:44.

duced early on, recurs as a visual motif of the film. Seeing the robust and commanding figure of Jesus reduced to wretchedness by men (or forces) who are obviously weaker—morally and physically—intensifies the tragedy of His suffering. Yet the contrast also contains certain logic. Somehow, even from the beginning, the viewer knows that Jesus is allowing this to happen. There must be a reason behind it.

A TALE OF TWO GARDENS

But what is the reason? What was the cause of His suffering and why did Jesus allow it? This question echoes in the viewer's mind like a silent refrain through the entire film. It rises to the surface only once, during the flagellation. Mary turns away from her suffering son, lifts her eyes to heaven and asks in a whisper, "My son … when, where, how will you choose to be delivered of this?" At that point Mary (and the viewer) question aloud the reason behind the extreme physical suffering Jesus must undergo. The suffering that begins in Gethsemane is different, though just as devastating. Jesus is being crushed by spiritual and moral suffering—the physical torture has not yet begun. But the question remains: why?

The Gospels themselves don't provide detailed explanations. They describe the facts: Jesus suffered; He suffered more than normal human beings can imagine; He suffered internally, and He also suffered physically and violently—most likely more violently than the film portrayed. Christian doctrine explains that Jesus suffered for sinners, for every sinner. That much is certain. Why the suffering had to be so intense is less apparent.

Yet the film fuses the rich streams of Christian reflection on Christ's suffering in Gethsemane into two evocative images, both of which share a common denominator: combat. The Garden of Gethsemane is the new Garden of Eden, the biblical place of testing and temptation, the place of spiritual battle described in Genesis. In the Garden of Eden, Adam (the biblical father of the human race) failed the test; in the face of the alluring, disconcerting, and threatening voice of evil, he let his trust in his Creator die in his heart. Arrogantly abusing his freedom, Adam disobeyed God. It was a crisis of faith, hope, and love that led to the human family's rebellion against God, what the Judeo-Christian tradition refers to as "original sin,"[4] or "the Fall." That sin, that lack of faith, hope, and love, let evil and suffering into human history; in a mysterious way it subjected the human family to the power of selfishness and sin, to the power of the Devil.

After the rebellion, God promised to send a Redeemer, a Savior who would free fallen mankind from the clutches of evil. To do so, the Savior would have to reverse Adam's disobedience. In the face of temptation, in the face of the alluring, disconcerting, and threatening voice of evil He would have to keep His trust in God firm; He would have to lovingly obey His divine Father no matter what.

Jesus, Christians believe, is that Redeemer. His Passion is the climax of His successful combat against the ancient enemy who had defeated Adam and subjected the human race to sin. Jesus' Passion is the definitive moment in history's dramatic struggle between good and evil.

THE NATURE OF THE BATTLE

Throughout the Passion, the combat takes the form of obedience versus suffering. The powers of darkness launch an assault first on Christ's inner life—here in the Garden—and then on His physical and relational life:

4 The Original Sin is most often labeled as a sin of pride understood as excessive self-aggrandizement. Instead of recognizing their own limits as finite creatures in dependence on a loving God (an attitude implicit in the great Christian virtues of faith, hope, and love), Adam and Eve tried to usurp God's own moral and metaphysical autonomy.

bodily torture, mockery, misunderstanding, and rejection at the hands of those He came to save. These sufferings were designed to break Christ's trust, to make Him turn His back on His Father, as Adam had done in Eden. His tormenters' cruelty escalates in its intensity: the powers of evil did everything possible to make Christ say, "Not Thy will be done, God, it's too hard; let Mine be done instead!" The Bible records that all of Adam's descendants had spoken out in just such a rebellion, following in the first parents' footsteps. If Jesus could endure far worse temptation and suffering than mankind had, and still stay faithful to His Father's will, still trust in God, then He would prove Himself stronger than the Prince of Darkness. He would usher in a New Creation, a New Era of reconciliation with God.

In *The Passion of The Christ*, nothing less was at stake. For this reason the New Testament has Christ Himself describing His Passion as the "hour" that belongs to the enemies of God: "But this is your [the Devil's] hour and the power of darkness."[5] In John's Gospel Jesus is even more explicit, referring directly to Satan as the one who has kept the human family subjected to suffering and sin ever since the disaster in the Garden of Eden: "I will not now speak many things with you," He tells His Apostles toward the end of their Last Supper together, "for the prince of this world cometh, and in me he hath not any thing."[6]

A COSMIC STRUGGLE

The film communicates this combat evocatively in dual sets of images. The first image is subtle, subconscious. There is an unnatural tension suffusing the elements of nature as you visually enter the garden. You hear a disturbing, otherworldly screech of a predatory bird, but you don't see it. You see

5 Luke 22:53.
6 John 14:30.

the moon obscured by clouds, then shining freely, then partly obscured, then blacked out—intentionally choreographed to reflect the inner struggle of Christ as He prays. You see a snake—in the Judeo-Christian tradition a symbol of Satan, Prince of Evil—slithering silently, seductively toward Jesus, trying to penetrate His world. (The snake used in the filming actually didn't try too hard. It kept slithering away from actor Jim Caviezel and meandering off camera. After numerous takes, the snake finally crawled over Jim's arms.)

This scene becomes a miniature incarnation of the immense battle between good and evil. It was a tricky thing to attempt. How do you depict such a grand struggle in such a tiny cinematic space and make it believable? One possibility would be to intersperse a quick succession of horrible images (like the atomic annihilation of Hiroshima, for instance, coupled with other terrible, sinful human atrocities). That documentary-type approach might have broken the dramatic tension, lessening the emotional edge. In a sense, it would have cheapened the whole struggle.

Such a critical scene had to communicate the gravity of the conflict and introduce the bigger battle without rupturing the personal intimacy of the moment for each person watching. As Christ desperately appeals to God, His Father, His cries become part of a mysterious conversation with natural phenomena happening around Him. Everything enters into Christ's internal combat: the moon, the clouds, the earth beneath Him. This is a vast, unfathomable struggle with Jesus caught in the middle, sweating drops of blood over it.

These cosmic elements insinuate the agonizing tug-of-war going on inside Jesus' soul. Theologians and spiritual writers generally agree that the struggle consisted of three essential dimensions, three main causes of Jesus' pain in Gethsemane.

THE BITTER AFTERTASTE OF SIN

First, Christ's suffering in the Garden was a unique internal experience of sin. Jesus Himself was free from sin. He had never given in to temptation and selfishness; He stayed faithful to the natural law and to God's will for Him personally all through His life. This sinlessness was an essential characteristic of the Savior, prefigured by the Old Covenant requirement that sacrifices offered in reparation for sin be animals "without blemish."[7] In Gethsemane, however, the evil of sin is poured into His soul. He is made the scapegoat[8] of all the sins that men and women had ever committed, and all the sins they were going to commit. He took upon Himself the responsibility for every act of betrayal and infidelity, every injustice, every crime against God, man, and nature perpetrated by the entire human race. Even people who are used to sinning feel agonizing remorse when faced with the true nature and consequences of their sinful actions. That gnawing, deadening weight of guilt was intensified almost beyond recognition in the pristine soul of the Savior, both because of His perfect love for God—which sin scorns—and because of the sheer quantity and atrocity of the crimes He was assuming. The New Testament attempts to describe this indescribable reality with a paradox: "Him [Christ], who knew no sin, he [God] hath made sin for us: that we might be made the justice of God in him." [9]

Later, St. Paul explains the paradox more fully, linking what happened in Gethsemane to the whole course of Christ's Passion: "And you [sinners],

7 e.g. Exodus 29:1.

8 Scapegoat is another Old Testament biblical symbol, a prefiguring (a type of prophecy) of the Savior, though the word has entered into common usage and lost its technical meaning. Each autumn when the Israelites celebrated the Day of Atonement they would perform various rituals of repentance for the sins they had committed as individuals and as a community during the previous year. One of these rituals consisted in sending into the wilderness a goat symbolically laden with those sins, thus separating the people from their sins and reestablishing their communion with God, which their sins had damaged or destroyed.

9 2 Corinthians 5:21.

when you were dead in your sins ... he [God] hath quickened together with him, forgiving you all offences. Blotting out the handwriting of the decree that was against us ... And he hath taken the same out of the way, fastening it to the cross."[10] In His Passion, which starts in Gethsemane, Christ took upon Himself the responsibility and consequences of all human sin.

For members of a fallen race, sin is a common occurrence and familiar companion, but for Christ, sin was "the scent and poison of death."[11] The mere vision of it would have repelled Him utterly. But this was no mere vision; it was a spiritual communion, a spiritual identification with the responsibility, the guilt of all those sins. Consequently, for Jesus, this was an indescribable inner torture.

Through the centuries, other artistic renditions of this biblical scene have depicted this unfathomable burden of sin more explicitly. Some show devils and demons mocking Jesus, an in-your-face parade of sin's grotesque-ness. Such arresting images communicate the theological meaning of the moment, but create an aura of otherworldliness around Christ's battle. Somehow, they come across as unreal, fairy-tale like images. To keep the struggle as visually real as possible—and perhaps, even more haunting—the film opts to accentuate the cosmic elements. The moon, the clouds, the earth are all caught up in a supernatural tension.

This artistic choice echoes the writers of the New Testament. They don't describe the details of why Christ was suffering in the Garden. But they do make an allusion to cosmic symbols. One of the Gospel writers, St.

10 Colossians 2:13-14.

11 John Henry Cardinal Newman, "Discourses to Mixed Congregations: Mental Sufferings of Our Lord in His Passion," quoted in Archbishop Goodier's *The Passion and Death of Our Lord Jesus Christ,* p. 156.

John, for example, marks the beginning of the Passion with three simple but heavily charged words: "It was night."[12]

THE TORMENT OF UNREQUITED LOVE

A second source of Christ's suffering in Gethsemane was His own privileged knowledge. Jesus knew how useless His self-sacrifice would be for the many individuals who would knowingly reject His offer of salvation. Jesus had nothing to gain personally from coming to earth and redeeming the human family. He did it solely out of love—a love for His Father who looked with mercy on the fallen human race. A love for every person caught in the vicious circle of selfishness. Jesus knew that sin doomed man to a deep, existential frustration. What every human heart needed above all else—intimate friendship with God—became unattainable.

Human beings were created to find meaning and fulfillment in that friendship, but original sin had shattered the possibility. Unless God renewed His offer of friendship and reached out a hand to heal those hearts mortally wounded by their compliance with evil, the world had no hope. Christ embodied the renewed offer of divine friendship with humankind. His hand could heal because it had never given in to evil. He did it out of an intense, knowing, personal love for each person. Yet during those agonizing hours in the Garden, most spiritual writers agree, God showed Jesus the countless people through the centuries who would refuse His offer and persist in their selfishness. That truth added inconsolable distress of unrequited love to the torture of biting remorse.

The film's visual depiction of this agony is captivating, but in reality it is a mere token of the suffering that must have really taken place. The Bible

---

12 John 13:30.

describes Christ's suffering as being "sorrowful unto death." What exactly could that mean? What is that feeling? What must that have been like? Artists—film directors included—tend to have a highly sensitive temperament, one that exacerbates their own sufferings and increases their capacity for empathy, but even their worst sufferings pale in comparison with what Christ must have experienced.

IN CONVERSATION WITH THE DEVIL

If the cosmic images allude to the magnitude of the combat going on, the movie's second set of images—the physical representation of Satan—focuses more on the personal dimension of Christ's inner battle: His one-on-one fight with the Devil. In the Garden of Eden, according to the Judeo-Christian tradition, the Devil instigated Adam and Eve's rebellion against God by engaging them in a little conversation. His words made them doubt God's goodness, stirred up envy, and made their healthy, humble obedience to their Creator seem like tyrannical slavery.

The New Testament makes dozens of references to Satan (the four Gospels mention him by name forty-eight times), but they don't mention him being present in the Garden of Gethsemane. Nevertheless, spiritual writers through the ages have interpreted Christ's description of His Passion as "your hour … the power of darkness"[13] to be a clear reference to the Devil's hand at work in the suffering and death of the Savior. The film picks this up and imaginatively reconstructs what the Devil's strategy would look like under these circumstances.

Just like in the Garden of Eden, Satan would have instigated a conversation, sowing tiny seeds of doubt and confusion, casting aspersions on

13 Luke 22:53.

the Father's goodness and instigating cynicism and rebellion. "Do you really believe that one man may bear the burden for all sin? ... No man can pay the price, I tell you. It is too high.... Ever. Never ... Who is your father?" In other words, just give it up, Jesus; all this suffering stuff isn't really going to work anyway.

It is a casual, not grotesque, personification of evil—another tactic communicating that a bigger battle was taking place.

REPELLING THE FIRST ATTACK

But there is a significant difference between the two Garden events. What happened in the Garden of Eden is not what unfolds in the Garden of Gethsemane. In Gethsemane, Jesus doesn't answer Satan, doesn't join in the conversation. He knows he's there, but He just shuts him out. In fact, Jesus doesn't even acknowledge Satan's presence until a startling cinematic moment when He stomps on the snake's head.

Instead of toying with temptation, Jesus rouses His trust. He engages all the powers of His soul to stay firmly anchored in His faith in God's goodness. Thus He is able to resist this first onslaught of evil and cling to His Father's will: "Shelter me, Lord. I place myself in your care, I place my trust in you."[14] Christ's faith and hope in God bring victory over evil.

Co-screenwriter Benedict Fitzgerald draws on an ancient Christian tradition here, depicting Christ using words from the Psalms, the "prayer book" of ancient Israel (still included in both the Jewish and the Christian Bibles), as Christ braces Himself for the final combat. Even though every fiber of His natural being is repelled by what His Father is asking Him to

14 That particular line is not a direct quotation from the Bible, but it uses language that appears again and again in the psalms, e.g. Psalm 27, 55, 31.

do ("Father … if it be possible, let this chalice pass from me...."), He is true to His love. Jesus' faith, hope, and trust remain firm ("but only Thy will be done, not mine").

The Gospels imply that the agony in the Garden lasted for at least an hour, and probably two or three hours. Jesus emerged victorious from this first wave of combat. His victory is graphically demonstrated in the film when Christ stands up decisively at the end of His prayer, crushing the serpent's head with a determined stamp of His foot. It's an image that fulfills the first Old Testament prophecy of the Savior.[15]

THE FRAILTY OF HUMAN NATURE

Taking all human sin upon Himself and knowing that, even so, many people would still reject His offer of salvation were, most spiritual writers agree, the first two causes of Christ's suffering in the Garden. The third cause was additional privileged information: Jesus knew beforehand, vividly and viscerally, all that He would have to go through in the next twelve hours—the humiliation, the betrayal, the rejection, the injustice, the imprisonment, the beatings, the flagellation, the torture, the mockery, the crucifixion, the death.

Considering the immensity of the first two burdens, this third burden can easily seem almost inconsequential. Nevertheless, Jesus Christ was a real man, a man in His thirties, in the prime of His life. Far from alleviating the indescribable disappointment and anxiety that any man would feel facing such a painful failure (at least, naturally speaking it was a failure), His divinity only enhanced it. His humanity was perfect, and therefore

---

15 Genesis 3:14-15: And the Lord God said to the serpent: Because thou hast done this thing, thou art cursed among all cattle, and beasts of the earth: upon thy breast shalt thou go, and earth shalt thou eat all the days of thy life. I will put enmities between thee and the woman, and thy seed and her seed: she shall crush thy head, and thou shalt lie in wait for her heel.

perfectly sensitive.

Precisely because of this third reason some people believe that the combat in the Garden must have been easy for Jesus. After all, He was the Son of God; He wasn't weak, ignorant, and selfish like your average human. Besides, He knew that His suffering would only last a little while, and then He would rise from the dead and reign forever. Sure He suffered, but not like us; He didn't really suffer the agony of doubt, despair, loneliness—all the real scourges of mankind's existential precariousness.

The reality of the Passion as narrated in the Gospels disagrees. Although the human mind has difficulty comprehending exactly how the Son of God could combine His special divine prerogatives with an authentic experience of absolute human misery, it is clear that He did. The Gospel writers use the strongest words they can find to describe the experience. The film follows suit. Every element of the scene is orchestrated to communicate agonizing mortal tension. Christ is given a full awareness of what He will endure, why, and for whom; Christ sees all the victories and losses; He sees the whole drama; He sees eternity.

Contemplating deeply and prayerfully the reasons behind His suffering can help the human heart accept the truth of its incomprehensible immensity. This is the common experience of saints and sinners alike through the centuries.

FREELY ACCEPTED

A final aspect of Christ's suffering, one that links it unmistakably to His love, is not often discussed: Jesus had the power to stop His suffering at any time. As the Son of God, He could have called down legions of angels to come to His defense,[16] but He didn't. He went through with it. In fact, Christ's

16 Cf. Matthew 26:53-54.

voluntary acceptance of His suffering is one reason it's so powerful. If He suffered so intensely, so wildly, it's only because He loved so intensely and wildly. That's why His wounds can heal.

If Christ had not truly suffered, and truly suffered terribly, in every way, then He would have been a cheap Savior. Only because He Himself walked in the darkest valleys, where the lost sheep cower in paralyzed despair, can He be the Good Shepherd of a fallen race. The New Testament describes this mysterious reality in the Epistle to the Hebrews, in a passage that especially calls to mind Christ's combat in Gethsemane:

> *Who in the days of his flesh, with a strong cry and tears, offering up prayers and supplications to him that was able to save him from death, was heard for his reverence. And whereas indeed he was the Son of God, he learned obedience by the things which he suffered. And being consummated, he became, to all that obey him, the cause of eternal salvation.*[17]

GETHSEMANE: A MICROCOSM OF THE WHOLE PASSION

In a sense, the rest of Christ's Passion simply unpacks what had already happened in the Garden of Gethsemane. The different genres of external suffering that accompany the rest of His Passion illustrate Jesus' inner agony. As He endures them, willfully mastering the instinctual resistance of His human nature ("let this chalice pass from me …"), His actions reiterate over and over again the words He prayed in the Garden, "I place my trust in you. … Father, only thy will be done, not mine.…"

Why so much suffering? It was the price love had to pay to ransom the lost beloved. Only heroic and loving obedience could untie the knot tied by Adam's tragic and selfish disobedience. Untying that knot is what

17 Hebrews 5:7-9.

Christ's Passion was all about, from the combat in the Garden until death on the Cross. Only in light of this cosmic dimension can one understand why this film is about "faith, hope, love, and forgiveness." Faith in the goodness of God, hope in the possibility of finding meaning in suffering, love that conquers death and evil, and forgiveness that flows out of the suffering Jesus endured. It is the only possible source of peace in a world shell-shocked by the violence of sin.

WHAT ABOUT THE ANGELS?

The New Testament adds a curious element to Christ's inner agony in Gethsemane. The Gospel of Luke describes how in the midst of it "there appeared to him an angel from heaven, strengthening him."[18] Jesus simply couldn't make it alone; His divine defenses were down and His human vulnerability was strained to the breaking point. He knew that, and so He asked Peter, James, and John to stay near Him and support Him, to watch with Him as He prayed and struggled. But they let Him down. They couldn't stay awake—all four Gospels record that tragic point. So God sent an angel to comfort Jesus instead.

In some of the early screenings, Christians familiar with the New Testament asked why the angels don't appear in the Gethsemane scene. It was another instance of the thousand-and-one choices Christian artists must make about how closely to follow the Gospel narratives. In this case, as in many others, the choice reflects a keen cinematic prudence. Because most people haven't seen angels, it would be hard to make them appear real. Reality and believability were absolutely essential.

A long-standing Christian belief explains exactly how the angel comforted Jesus at that critical time. Jesus sees in that moment not only all those

18 Luke 22:43.

who would reject His offer of salvation, but also all those who would accept it, who would respond to His love by giving love back. The common Christian view of Gethsemane admits that every person's sins were there, tormenting the Lord, but repentant sinners were also there, comforting Christ with their acts and efforts of fidelity.

Being able to comfort the heart of Jesus by repenting from sins, battling selfishness, and staying faithful to one's friendship with God has been one of the great motivations for Christians since the first days of the Church. In a sense, all Christians join ranks with the sleepy Apostles when they let their tendencies to self-indulgence and egoism lead them sinfully astray from the path of Christ's self-sacrificing love. But they can just as truly "stay awake" with Him by their efforts to follow Him, to love selflessly, as He did.

In this sense, the Passion of Christ is also a pattern of Christian living extended to everyone to follow. Christians don't believe that Christ saved the world by eliminating evil, sin, and suffering (that's evident from today's news stories). Rather, He conquered them from within—He loved and trusted, He hoped and believed in spite of them. Friendship with Christ plugs the human heart back into the source of divine grace that can help all people do the same thing. It enables individuals to grow in spiritually and morally, so that they can extend Christ's conquest in their own lives. Destructive human disobedience and sin, whether on a personal or social scale, can be reversed just as Christ reversed the disobedience of Adam's original sin. This is one reason why the quintessential Christian prayer, the "Our Father" or "Lord's Prayer" taught by Christ Himself, echoes the prayer uttered by Christ in the moment of His most intense contest against evil: "…Thy Kingdom come, Thy will be done [not mine, tainted as it is by selfishness] on earth as it is in heaven."

deeper. He, along with many of his contemporaries (and the other Apostles), envisioned the promised Savior as someone who would reestablish the earthly glory of King David's reign, making Israel once again a political force to be reckoned with on the international scene,[20] maybe into the most powerful of nations. Jesus did speak frequently about the coming of His Kingdom. His miracles and incomparable charisma made it seem as if He could indeed pick up where David and Solomon had left off in Israel's heyday, the tenth-century B.C.

Being a member of Christ's inner circle was attractive to Judas as long as this remained a real possibility. But Judas seemed to perceive more quickly than the other Apostles that Jesus had something else in mind. Judas understood that Christ's Kingdom was "not of this world,"[21] as Jesus Himself would later explain to Pontius Pilate during His trial. When this became clear, Judas was forced to choose: would he adhere to Jesus and his otherworldly Kingdom, or would he launch out on his own to climb the ladder of worldly wealth and influence?

THE REAL JUDAS

Judas can too easily be written off as wholly evil, the paradigm of absolute corruption. In truth, however, every person has to face that same choice in life, many times; it is a very real choice, and Judas is a very real person. Often the choice doesn't appear particularly religious—just the tug of one's conscience, for instance, to resist easy pleasure and glittery success. It's a prodding of one's heart to stay faithful to the things that really matter, the things that last—friendships, family, faith, justice. Often the choice even seems blasé, insignificant, whereas Judas' choice was dramatic, of enormous scope—

20 Around the year 1000 B.C. David had united the tribes of Israel into a formidable kingdom, which he passed on to his son, Solomon.

21 Cf. John 18:36: Jesus answered, My kingdom is not of this world. If my kingdom were of this world, my servants would certainly strive that I should not be delivered to the Jews. But now my kingdom is not from hence.

at least in hindsight. For these reasons, labeling Judas as the paradigm of extreme corruption can be a slick tactic to deceive oneself into belittling the weight of everyday moral choices and deadening one's conscience.

The film opted for a different Judas. Even as he appears before the leaders of Jerusalem to close the despicable deal, he seems unsure of himself, visibly anxious. The Jewish priests Caiaphas and Annas show no compassion; they are convinced that Jesus needs to be apprehended, but they recognize that Judas' betrayal is a dishonorable deed. They don't hand the money to Judas; they throw it at him, like a bone to a dog. The film's slow motion flight of the coins—symbol of all the worldly glamour, pleasure, and influence that money makes accessible—and their collision with Judas, who can't hold on to them, who is almost accosted by them, emphasizes both the attraction of earthly glory and its insubstantiality. The coins shine and sparkle, but they are cold and hard; you hear the harsh metal clanking on the stone floor as they spill to the ground. As Judas hurriedly gathers the coins both his greed and his anxiety are evident. When the guards close in around him, Judas stops momentarily and looks worriedly up at them—the perfect icon of a torn conscience. He is no archetype of evil; he is just like you and me.

Judas is complex. On the one hand, he recognized that Jesus was setting Himself up for a confrontation with the political and religious leaders of Israel, a confrontation that He might or might not win. But Judas wasn't ready to burn all his bridges with the power elite. If Jesus lost the confrontation, His faithful followers might end up washed away in the wake of Jesus' failure. On the other hand, even if Judas threw his chips in with Jesus' enemies, if Jesus won the confrontation, He would always accept Judas back into the coterie—after all, the Lord was the paragon of forgiveness. So Judas hedged his bets.

He arranged the secret betrayal with a hefty price, so that, win or lose, he would come out with something in the bank. Still, he wasn't too proud of himself. He didn't want to broadcast what he was doing. He didn't like the idea of being seen as a traitor in front of his friends. All these conflicting emotions and motivations were present in the film's portrayal of Judas. And because he was so complex, he was real, a tragic character that viewers could identify with. That's exactly the point.

AN UNSURPRISING TRAGEDY

The Old Testament prophesied the betrayal of the Savior.[22] In the time of the ancient Hebrew Patriarchs (circa 1800 B.C.), envy drove Jacob's ten older sons to sell his eleventh son (their half-brother), Joseph, into slavery. They too did it for a handful of silver pieces. God in His Providence used that betrayal for the good of Jacob's family—Joseph ended up becoming viceroy of Egypt and saving his brothers and their whole clan during a famine.[23] The brothers were reconciled, and they became the heads of the Twelve Tribes of Israel, God's Chosen People. In a similar way, Christians believe, God's Providence turned Judas' betrayal into the source of salvation for all people; Christ's self-sacrifice provided the "bread of life"[24] that would relieve the spiritual famine created by original sin.

Christians also see Judas' betrayal referred to prophetically in the Book of Psalms. Many spiritual writers even see in these passages (and others) an indication that the greatest suffering Christ endured throughout His Passion was, in fact, Judas' betrayal. A passage from Psalm 54 is often referred to as an especially poignant prefiguring of Christ's sentiments in

22 The prophet Zechariah even alludes to the price of the rejection being thirty pieces of silver, the amount of the payment Judas received (typical price of a slave at the time). Cf. Zechariah, chapter 11.

23 You can read the remarkable story in Genesis 37-48.

24 Jesus said to them, I am the bread of life; he who comes to me shall not hunger, and he who believes in me shall never thirst (John 6:35).

relation to this aspect of His Passion:

> *For if my enemy had reviled me, I would verily have borne with it. And*
> *if he that hated me had spoken great things against me, I would perhaps*
> *have hidden my self from him. But thou a man of one mind, my guide,*
> *and my familiar, who didst take sweetmeats together with me, in the*
> *house of God we walked with consent....*[25]

Psalm 40 expresses the same sorrow:

> *All my enemies whispered together against me; they devised evils to me.*
> *... For even the man of my peace, in whom I trusted, who ate my bread,*
> *hath greatly supplanted me.*[26]

Those descriptions are hardly the epitome of monstrous evil; the film is true to Scripture when it portrays Judas as a complex character indeed.

The New Testament discreetly reiterates the severe wound Judas' betrayal made in the heart of Christ. During the Last Supper, the Passover Seder that Jesus celebrated with His Apostles the night before His Passion, Jesus referred to it explicitly: "When Jesus had said these things, he was troubled in spirit; and he testified, and said: Amen, amen, I say to you, one of you shall betray me."[27]

WHAT JESUS THOUGHT OF JUDAS

And yet, to the end Jesus held out the hand of friendship to His betrayer. The film first portrays this in the way Jesus looks at Judas in the Garden. As the soldiers enter Gethsemane Jesus stands forth, ready to fulfill His Father's

25 Psalm 54:13-15.

26 Psalm 40:8, 10.

27 John 13:21.

will. Judas had arranged to identify Jesus by greeting Him with a kiss, a common salutation and sign of friendship in first-century Palestine. (Some kind of sign was necessary because in the dark the guards may have had difficulty identifying Jesus, or one of Jesus' disciples may have tried to pass himself off as Jesus in order to provide a chance for their leader's escape.) When Judas sees Jesus and the other Apostles, his initial reaction is to flee. Judas was clearly ashamed of himself in front of his friends, in front of the other Apostles he knew so well. But the guards force Judas to follow through with his plan.

As he moves towards Jesus, you see close-ups of John and Peter, representatives of the other Apostles, looking at Judas with sheer contempt. In contrast, the face of Jesus is welcoming, warm, and sincere till the end. His response to the betrayal, when He says sadly, "Judas, dost thou betray the Son of man with a kiss?"[28], is more a gentle call to repentance than a stinging accusation. The film emphasizes Jesus' mercy and love in a subsequent scene. Jesus and Judas meet again, in a surprising way, after the arrest. Judas is cowering in a cave beneath a bridge. As Jesus is being dragged back to the city, the soldiers knock Him off the bridge, and His bruised, contorted face looks over at Judas trembling in the cave. Even then, Jesus gives no sign of condemnation, no indication of anger or resentment. Even then, He is open, inviting Judas to repent.

The Gospels don't record that encounter, though the movie's depiction makes it appear possible, even probable. And if it didn't occur physically to Judas, it certainly occurred spiritually (God always invites sinners to repentance).

It's probable that on the trip back to Jerusalem, when Jesus was

28 Luke 22:48.

chained and bound, the guards were slapping and punching Him. In her meditations on the Lord's Passion, published after her death as *The Dolorous Passion of Our Lord Jesus Christ*, Sister Anne Catherine Emmerich, a nineteenth-century German nun and mystic, narrates that such blows knocked Him off a bridge. The film adds the encounter with Judas, hiding under the bridge. Judas has taken the money, he has turned Jesus over to the enemy by kissing Him, and then he flees. He runs away to hide, because he feels awful about what he's done. He's scared; he's done something very wrong; he's betrayed his best friend. So there he is, under the bridge, trying to hide from the truth of his horrendous deed.

But you can't hide from the truth; you can't escape from it. Judas ends up going right to the place where he will have to come face-to-face with it. Jesus is the truth. When He gets knocked off the bridge, and Judas sees Him, for a moment, it looks like Judas is trying to say something, to ask for forgiveness, to apologize. His mouth tries to form the words, but they don't come out. He can't bring himself to admit his failure, to accept the truth. And then the moment of opportunity passes and the soldiers pull Jesus back up to the bridge.

Immediately afterward Judas sees a demon, a monstrous creature—it's a manifestation of the pangs of his conscience and the torment of the Devil rolled into one. He can't face that either, he has to run away from it. At that point, however, the audience suspects that he's not going to get away. He has abandoned the freedom that comes from living in harmony with truth; that freedom has abandoned him.

THE TRAGIC END OF JUDAS

The next time Judas is on screen is during Jesus' first trial in front of the Jewish leaders in Jerusalem. Watching from the back of the crowd, Judas becomes more distressed at what is happening to Jesus. Under the cover of darkness, he seeks out the high priest, Caiaphas, in order to return the thirty pieces of blood money and plead for Jesus' release. Even then he can't accept responsibility for his betrayal. Judas could have come back to Jesus at any time, he could have wept for his sins and Jesus would have forgiven him. But he doesn't come back.

That's the remarkable thing about human freedom. God won't force-feed His love; Judas was just too proud to accept his failings and the forgiveness that he needed. Letting oneself be loved even when one is unworthy of love requires humility. Many people, like Judas, simply refuse to take that step. That's the real tragedy of Judas, not that he betrayed Christ, but that he didn't trust in Christ's forgiveness.

The forces of evil—led by Satan—torment Judas, trying to prevent his regret from maturing into humble repentance. Using the demonic children was another way to manifest the film's conception of evil as something good gone horribly wrong. The children connote innocence, loyalty, docility; the demonic twist connotes lost innocence, lost loyalty, lost docility—losses that Satan uses to drive Judas to the brink of despair. When the moment of decision comes, however, the Devil disappears, the children disappear, and Judas is left alone, free either to take the last step on his frantic and useless flight away from the truth, or to entrust himself to God's mercy. The only thing he sees is a maggot-infested donkey carcass, its white teeth gleaming in the morning sunlight (an explicit allusion to Hell, which the New Testament refers to as a place where there is "gnashing of teeth" and where "the worms die not"[29]). The sight pushes Judas over the edge. He begins to sob, and then he yields to despair.

This is one of the most haunting scenes of the film. Perhaps all the

29 Cf. Matthew 13:50 and Mark 9:47.

most powerful scenes share the characteristics of this one: they are scenes where everything is communicated just by a look, where you forget all the dialogue and abstract concepts and you confront the raw human experience. When you see Judas begin to sob, after cutting back and forth between his anguished face and the rotting face of the donkey, you know he has run out of hope.

It took a little while to get the drama right on this scene. In the end, Luca Lionello (the actor who played Judas) received the signal to look at the rotting donkey, with the maggots and the flies crawling out its nose, and imagine that the rotting beast was luckier than he was. He was directed to think that he would prefer to be that donkey, rather than what he was. Only then did Luca get it. On the next take he started to cry, and the tears kept coming.

PETER: THE OTHER SIDE OF THE JUDAS COIN

The parallel to Judas is Peter, one of Jesus' closest disciples. During the trial with Caiaphas, Peter, too, is in the crowd watching. When some threatening bystanders accuse him of being one of Jesus' followers, he vehemently denies even knowing Jesus. This happens three times. He has betrayed Jesus too. Though similar to Judas, there are definite differences between the actions of the two men clearly found in the Gospels.

Peter's emotions are not complicated: he was simply terrified. He saw what was going on and he thought, *Uh oh, I'm next. I'll have my head on the chopping block, and I'm not ready for this....* He hadn't received the courage of the Holy Spirit yet. Peter's denial came out of his weakness. Caught off guard in a moment of confusion, he didn't think about it and prepare for it as Judas had done. He just fell into it. This is why Peter was able to recover when Jesus gave Him that indescribable look after Peter's third denial. Judas had seen the same look from Jesus too, but he had already hardened his heart.

Judas had his moment of truth when Jesus fell off the bridge and gave him one last look, one last invitation to repentance. Peter's opportunity comes after his third denial. Jesus falls to the ground under the blows of His captors and turns His head to Peter, who has also fallen to the ground. The camera shots of Jesus' two looks are uncannily similar. The difference was in the responses of the two disciples. Judas had already hardened his heart too much; Peter hadn't. Realizing what has happened, Peter flees. A moment later when he runs into Mary, Peter finds the strength to accept his failure, to repent, to admit his sin. Mary's look echoes Jesus', and she accepts Peter's repentance in Jesus' place, since Peter can't get to Jesus to ask directly.

The Gospels don't record this specific encounter between Mary and Peter, but it emphasizes the contrast between Peter and Judas, bringing into sharper relief the message of hope taught by Christ's reactions to the betrayals. Anne Catherine Emmerich envisioned Mary being in the crowd, which is feasible, as is an encounter between Mary and Peter. The artistic sensibility intuits that Mary would have gravitated to him. That was Peter's moment to be confronted by the truth, and to respond to it, to accept it. Judas, on the other hand, simply saw Jesus and froze. He was caught in the Hell of his own moral paralysis. Jesus would have forgiven him, but Judas' disposition wasn't right; Peter's was. It's the mystery of human freedom—an essential theme in all four Gospels—showcased by the film because of its essential link to love and forgiveness.

What saved Peter from despair, why did he have the "right disposition" and Judas didn't? The flashback after Peter's denial provides a clue. Jesus had predicted Peter's denial at the Last Supper (the scene of the flashback), just as He had predicted Judas' betrayal, according to the Gospel narratives. Peter realizes that the prediction has come true. As he looks into Christ's bruised and swollen eyes, it dawns on Peter that Jesus knew all along how weak he really was, how arrogant and conceited. And yet, even knowing that, Jesus never pulled back His love. Becoming aware of Christ's immeasurable love for him, Christ's unconditional love for him—that's what saved Peter from despair. Christ's love bred Peter's hope.

GOOD GUILT, BAD GUILT

Peter's denial was as equally heartwrenching for Peter as Judas' was for Judas. Early Christian tradition relates that Peter wept for that denial every day for the rest of his life. But Peter used it as a springboard to grow in love and trust. It taught him that he was weak, and he accepted the lesson, along with Christ's forgiveness. Judas didn't.

The film's insight into Judas' tragic passage to despair fits in with the great spiritual writers' understanding of the moral life. Human nature has a built-in moral gauge that impels you to adhere to what is right and avoid or reject what is wrong. Although the gauge has been damaged by original sin (and sometimes social and cultural influences aggravate the damage), it still points toward behavior characterized by traits like fairness, loyalty, and generosity. The impetus to do good and avoid evil (discerning between the two is often where the damage makes things difficult) makes itself felt more acutely at two moments of every moral decision: just before and just after.

Temptations (moral interference transmitted by the forces of evil and their leader, the Devil) frequently come at those moments as well. Before the moment of decision temptations supply reasons and alternatives against choosing what is morally right. Sometimes those reasons and alternatives present an almost irresistible force, as during Christ's combat in Gethsemane.

After the decision has been made, when the moral gauge is registering approval for a good decision or disapproval for a bad one, temptations change their tack. In the aftermath of a good decision, they often retreat to gather strength for another onslaught. In the aftermath of a bad decision, they often conjure feelings of self-deprecation and hopelessness. The moral courage necessary to admit one's failings is drained off. A person accepts no responsibility for the wrong done.

Guilt is the name given to the moral gauge's indication that a wrong decision has been made. In itself, guilt is morally neutral: it can lead either to repentance (as in the case of Peter) or to flight and denial (as in the case of Judas). Feeling guilt is a sign that the moral gauge, however damaged it may be, is still operating—the first requirement for any kind of moral or truly spiritual life. What each person does with that guilt will determine his or her moral character and spiritual strength. In the end, everyone can be like Peter, and everyone can be like Judas.

THE ARREST

The moment when the Temple guards take hold of Jesus marks the beginning of His physical Passion: the humiliation of His person and torture of His body. In the Garden, when Jesus halts the brief skirmish between the guards and the Apostles, and miraculously cures Malchus's severed ear, His uncanny composure and air of command reiterate the freedom with which He was accepting all that was to come. Even the soldiers clearly recognize that if He wanted to He could easily overcome them. As they lay hands on Him, they do so cautiously. Only when they see with their own eyes that He is putting up absolutely no resistance does their cowardly bravado return— and with a vengeance, as they buffet their victim all the way back to the city. Jesus knew the price God was asking Him to pay to redeem the human race, and He freely paid it.

The Gospel narratives emphasize the same message—the freedom of Christ's self-sacrifice—in various ways. St. Matthew records Jesus' argument for convincing Peter to drop his sword: "Thinkest thou that I cannot ask my Father, and he will give me presently more than twelve legions [72,000] of angels? How then shall the scriptures be fulfilled, that so it must be done?"[30] St. John goes into more detail. He records the dialogue in which Jesus questions the guards about whom they are searching for. They answer "Jesus of Nazareth," and Jesus responds: "I am he," just as it occurs in the film. But then St. John adds a strange detail: "As soon therefore as he had said to them, 'I am he,' they went backward and fell to the ground."[31] The force of His identity simply bowls them over (the words "I am he" correspond in the original language to God's holy name as revealed to Moses 1,500 years earlier and recorded in the book of Exodus; it was a name that the Israelites were forbidden to pronounce except once a year, when the High Priest performed the rites of atonement).

All Christians believe this happened, since it is recorded in the New Testament, but how could you depict such a scene in a way that strikes viewers as real, which was so essential to this film? In the Bible it happens before anyone starts grabbing or jostling or anything; it's an entirely supernatural event. Depicting it could easily have distracted people, shocking them in the wrong way; it was better to make everything—especially so early in the film—believable.

Even so, an interesting coincidence occurred during the filming. That sequence was shot in pieces, creating a stylistic impression rather than a logical one. The cameras went in close on the action, without choreographing the whole thing so you knew where everyone was all the time. Utilizing

30 Matthew 26:53-54.
31 John 18:6.

very slow movements, the focus is on the actors' eyes, and their uncertain exchanges of glances. It became a "Who's going make the first move?" type of
approach. You see one person look at another person and you wonder what's
going on. Then you see other figures walking out of the woods. The encounter comes together slowly; it almost makes sense, but not quite.

The wide shots were filmed last. After all the close-ups, they pulled
back to shoot from a distance. That's when the odd coincidence happened.
Everyone was directed to take their places wherever they happened to end
up at the end of the unchoreographed skirmish. When the actors took their
positions, everyone was on the ground except Jesus, who remained in the
center of the melee, standing there, alone, peacefully, with all the soldiers on
the ground in front of Him, just as it happens in the Gospel. The detail had
been consciously extracted from the screenplay, but it made its way back in
of its own accord. What had been purposely avoided in favor of believability
had actually happened. Jesus' superhuman strength and composure made it
on screen in spite of everything. Somehow, it was necessary to emphasize the
freedom with which He suffered His Passion, because freedom is an essential
element of love, and the Passion is all about love.

AN EMPHASIS ON FREEDOM

Jesus' free acceptance of the suffering He underwent in His Passion in spite
of having the power to avoid it distinguishes it from the rest of human suffering. Some skeptics compare the Passion with the horrendous tortures
endured by prisoners of war or other victims of unspeakable violence. The intensity of the physical pain, the utter humiliation, and the psycho-emotional
affliction are indeed comparable. That is one reason why people through the
centuries have been able to find God's presence even in the midst of atrocious suffering—they know that He experienced it too. But if prisoners of
war and other victims had been able to call down twelve legions of angels to

free themselves from their torturers, they would have. Many of these men and women have suffered (and are even now suffering) courageously, even heroically. But Christ suffered His atrocities voluntarily from start to finish, accepting them even though He had the power to avoid them.

One of the earliest surviving Christian liturgical texts, a third-century Eucharistic prayer (i.e. the prayer surrounding the narration of the Last Supper used by the Catholic priest during the sacrifice of the Mass), places special emphasis on this aspect of the Passion: "Before he was given up to death, *a death he freely accepted* …" It was the freedom with which Christ accepted the "cup of suffering" that made it redemptive. He did not deserve to suffer; He had never taken part in the cause of suffering—sin, evil, selfishness. Yet He freely accepted it, out of love for the Father and love for every human soul. "Put up thy sword back into the scabbard," He says to Peter in the Garden, and St. John records how He finished the statement, "The chalice which my Father hath given me, shall I not drink it?"[32] It is the bitter cup of suffering that would become the sweet cup of salvation.

LOVE AND SUFFERING

His uniquely free acceptance of suffering transformed suffering—an evil in itself, a consequence of sin—into an instrument of salvation. Salvation is linked to love, and love means self-giving. Self-giving, in a world inundated with self-indulgence and within a human nature skewed towards self-centeredness, always involves some kind of suffering, some kind of self-denial. This is how Christ defined love, as self-sacrifice for the sake of the beloved. Undergoing His Passion was one way to make sure His disciples understood exactly what He meant, to give them a visual icon of authentic love:

---

32 John 18:11.

This is my commandment, that you love one another, as I have loved you. Greater love than this no man hath, that a man lay down his life for his friends. You are my friends, if you do the things that I command you.... By this shall all men know that you are my disciples, if you have love one for another.[33]

In Christ's Passion, the redeeming obedience which reversed original sin and overcame the forces of evil also reversed the meaning of human suffering. From then on, any human suffering accepted with faith and hope, and thereby united to Christ's suffering, could share in the redemptive power of the Savior's redeeming self-sacrifice. To witness the Passion without keeping that in mind is to miss a large part of the point.

LESSONS FROM MALCHUS

When Christ is apprehended, the violence and betrayal and brutality exit Gethsemane, yet the film offers a curious final image in the Garden. Malchus, a member of the arresting mob, is sitting on the ground, touching his ear, utterly stunned. Only minutes before he had been the ringleader of the cruel and ruthless Temple guards. Now he is simply incapable of following them back into the city. His experience in the Garden has yanked him into another world. That man, Jesus, that rabble-rousing rabbi whom they had been sent to arrest, had miraculously restored the bloody and painful mess of his severed ear. Malchus was the recipient of a miracle; a supernatural gift bestowed by this Jesus on an enemy, on a man sworn to apprehend Him unjustly in the middle of the night. This was no ordinary rabbi; this was no ordinary Garden; this was no ordinary night. Not for Malchus.

33 John 15:12-14; 13:35.

The film emphasized that small miracle because it is so eloquent. It shows what Jesus was really about. He was on a different level. He was God, and He let Himself be taken prisoner by ignoble men. He even healed one of them. It's a moment that all sinners who have experienced Christ's forgiveness appreciate deeply. In the midst of chaos and injustice and violence, Jesus displays gentle mercy for His enemy. The contrast is not only emotionally moving, but theologically significant and instructive. The film had to show an icon of composure and equilibrium and goodness in a maelstrom of passion and cutting and slashing, because Christians want to be able to live it. It's part of the story, a particularly expressive part.

It is said that Malchus became a Christian and joined the early Church in Jerusalem. Changing from a servant of violence and injustice into a defender of truth and peace is maybe more miraculous than replacing a severed ear; the film shows that Christ's Passion has the power for both. That's another reason why this movie is about hope.

CHAPTER 3

⟶ ✠ ⟵

TRIAL IN THE TEMPLE

MARY'S SECRET

In the Garden of Eden, Adam wasn't alone; Eve was with him. Scripture refers to Christ as the new Adam, who through His "becoming obedient unto death, even to the death of the cross"[34] became the father of redeemed humanity, just as the first Adam through his disobedience had become the father of a fallen humanity. In a similar way, some ancient Christian writers refer to Mary, Christ's mother, as a kind of second Eve. God had created the human race "in his own image, male and female he created them."[35] And when the human race fell into sin, it fell together, male and female, Adam and Eve. It was appropriate therefore that when it was to be redeemed by a new Adam another "Eve" should have a role to play as well—though only a secondary role. It was this role that the prophet Simeon had referred to when he first beheld the child Jesus in the Temple and he told Mary, "Behold, this child is set for the fall and for the resurrection of many in Israel, and for a

34 Philippians 2:8.

35 Genesis 1:27.

sign which shall be contradicted. And thy own soul a sword shall pierce."[36]

Mary probably knew more clearly than anyone besides Jesus Himself what would happen in Jesus' Passion and why. Spiritual writers have commented on this theologically, but the film takes a common sense approach; it suggests that they talked about more things than just the weather during all those years together in Nazareth. Her recognition of Jesus' arrest as a "beginning" implies that she knew everything that was going to unfold, at least in broad strokes. She knew something important and terrible was coming, because Jesus would have told her about it. Maybe He didn't give her the whole story, because she couldn't have borne it. But she knew something big was coming, and she was prepared for it. It was a sacrifice, His sacrifice, and that was why He had come. She knew it. It was Mary's secret.

A MOTHER'S HEART

The emotional and spiritual union between Mary and Jesus is another of the film's recurring themes. Its first occurrence takes place on the threshold of the trial. As soon as Jesus is arrested, the camera cuts abruptly to the room where Mary is staying. She wakes up violently, as if she herself has been taken captive. She knows that the Passion has begun, and she expresses her intuition by reciting the first words of the Jewish Passover Seder ceremony: "Why is this night unlike every other night?" Mary Magdalene, her companion and one of Jesus' most devoted followers, gives the proper ceremonial response: "Because once we were slaves and now we are slaves no longer … on this night we were led from captivity to freedom."

The Passover Seder is an annual Jewish holiday commemorating ancient Israel's liberation from slavery in Egypt, the people "passing over"

36 Luke 2:34-35.

from slavery to freedom. This liberation was accompanied by signs and portents that God performed through His servant Moses (like the parting of the Red Sea).[37] One of the most vivid symbols of this Passover was the sacrificial lamb. To convince Pharaoh to release the Hebrew captives into the desert where they could worship freely, God sent a series of ten plagues on Egypt. The last—and most severe—was the plague that killed Egypt's firstborn sons. The Hebrew families were spared this plague through specific instructions from God—they were told to sprinkle the blood of a sacrificial lamb on the doorway of their houses and the angel of death, seeing the blood, would pass over. The lamb that was sacrificed the day before was eaten in a symbolic meal that evening. The lamb was called the "Paschal" lamb, the "Passover" lamb, and became a central symbol of the Old Covenant (i.e. God's ancient promise to send Israel a Savior, a Messiah).

Christians see in this miraculous liberation from physical slavery a prefiguring of humanity's liberation from the slavery of sin. They see in the Paschal Lamb a prefiguring of Christ Himself (whom the New Testament repeatedly calls "the lamb of God"[38]), the firstborn Son of God sacrificed as a victim for the sins of all mankind in order to save them from eternal death. The night before His Passion, Jesus celebrated what is called the Last Supper—His last Passover Seder. During the meal, He announced the establishment of a New Covenant, one that He would seal with His own blood instead of a lamb's. From then on, His blood would become the tangible expression of the redeeming love that motivated His self-sacrifice, as well as the real instrument of that redemption—just as the lamb's blood had been a symbol of and instrument for Israel's salvation from Egypt.

All this is evoked by Mary's recitation of that one line in the film.

37 See the Book of Exodus, chapters 6-15.
38 Cf. John 1:29.

The line wasn't in the original screenplay. It was actor Maia Morgenstern's (who played Mary) own idea. Maia is a believing, practicing Jew, familiar with the rituals and symbolism of the Passover Seder. When they were filming this scene, she asked if she could add that line. It fit perfectly. Jesus' arrest—bound and chained—paralleled the binding of the Paschal Lamb before it was sacrificed; in a sense, Mary's line summarizes all the messianic prophecies.

In later flashbacks in the film, the relationship between the Last Supper and the Passion are more explicitly linked—in fact, the Paschal Lamb was even the theme of some flashbacks that didn't make it out of the editing room. What comes across in this first allusion, though, is Mary's deep union with Christ. She shares His suffering in her own motherly soul right from the start. Following Christ's lead, she too freely accepts it as part of His Father's plan for the redemption of fallen humanity. "It has begun, my Lord; so be it," she prays when she gets her first glimpse of the fettered Jesus.

THE WISDOM OF A MOTHER'S SORROW

Accepting the Father's will wasn't easy for either one of them. Christ's acceptance didn't lessen the agony He endured in Gethsemane. Not the pain that racked Him as His face and body were gradually torn to shreds, nor the loneliness that invaded His heart as His closest disciples and friends abandoned Him. Mary's suffering was more intimate and hidden, but still visible, even in these early stages. When Christ has been condemned and He is waiting, chained in a dungeon, to be taken to Pontius Pilate for sentencing, Mary is drawn to Him. She can't see which cell they have taken Him to, but her mother's love doesn't need to see; she simply knows.

As she kneels to caress the stones that imprison her son, the depths of her sorrow penetrate them, and reach down into Jesus' heart. Perhaps it comforted and strengthened Him in that moment; perhaps it made His own suffering worse, knowing that His mother's Passion had finally begun as well. Christians have always taken courage from the deep suffering Mary shared with Jesus. Her example shows that Christian joy doesn't depend on feelings and circumstances, but on love—an authentic love that even the deep waters of suffering can't extinguish.

Mary's intimate participation in Christ's sufferings has been one source of her unique place in Christian devotion. By baptism, Christians believe, men and women become Christ's brothers and sisters; they enter into God's family as adopted children. Since Mary was Christ's mother, she also becomes the spiritual mother of Christians. Just as her tender and deep mother's love led her to share in Christ's sufferings and thereby accompany Him in a way that gave Him strength and comfort, so too she accompanies Christians in their sufferings. Mary and Christ's hearts are united, eloquently depicted in the film by the single camera shot that dissolves their physical separation; this also expresses the union of hearts between Mary and Christians.

THE FIRST FLASHBACK

When Jesus enters the site of His first trial, He sees a carpenter at work nearby. The screenplay notes that this carpenter was part of a group who were hurriedly constructing Jesus' cross in anticipation of His execution. Another scene with Judas helping the guards pick out the wood for the cross was also in the screenplay. These scenes, garnered from various spiritual authors, were filmed but left on the cutting room floor. The scenes were beautiful, but distractions from the real story. In the end, the closer the film followed the Gospel narratives, the more streamlined and powerful the drama.

Seeing the carpenter takes Jesus mentally back to His days as a carpenter in Nazareth. This is the first of a series of flashbacks used both to emphasize the meaning behind certain aspects of the Passion, and also to give visual relief to the viewer from the onscreen brutality. The flashback is bittersweet, however; when you come back, the brutality is even more jarring.

This first flashback serves a clear purpose. Mary has just made her initial appearance, but the audience doesn't really know her identity. Seeing her at home with her son—fixing lunch, gently chiding Him as mothers do—tells the audience who she is, and how real and close their relationship was. Add to that the visual brightness of the flashback, which takes place during the day, and the clean, vigorous appearance of Jesus, and you easily share the horror that Mary must feel when she sees Jesus bleeding, bruised, and in chains. The viewer enters effortlessly into her compassion.

Watching the film for the second or third time, you realize the necessity to show the flashback. When Mary first appears in the film, startled awake, you don't quite know who she is yet. You surmise that it must be Jesus' mother—there's an unspoken connection when their eyes meet as He's being dragged into the trial. The flashback lets you see them together during a normal day in the backyard. He's there at the workbench making a table, and she's fixing lunch. They laugh together and are affectionate. There's a deep relationship between them.

JESUS CHRIST: A REAL MAN

The Nazareth flashback has another message—Jesus' humanity. Even Christians are tempted to forget that Jesus was truly man as well as truly God. He lived a normal, working-man's life for thirty years in a backwater town on the outskirts of the Roman Empire. He had a sense of humor, He had to sweat to make a living, His mother told Him to wash his hands before eating …

He was really one of us.[39] This is the central truth of Christian revelation, known as the dogma of the Incarnation, the "becoming flesh" (the etymological meaning of *incarnation*) of God. True, because He was the Son of God He was *more* than we, but at the same time, because He was truly incarnate, He was *no less* than we. Thus, for Christians, Jesus is not only the divine Savior, but also a brother, a friend, and a model for living. It is a concept of the divinity unique to Christianity. God became a human child, born of Mary, in order to show all people how to live as children of God. This was the precondition for His Passion—if He hadn't been truly human, He wouldn't have been able truly to suffer. The Incarnation too, therefore, is an act of love that can fill the heart with hope.

After some of the early screenings of the film audience members questioned why Jesus is seen building a modern table. It's primarily comic relief. The implication is that since He was God He would know all about modern table and chair designs, even though they hadn't been invented yet. Or perhaps that as a perfect man His exceptional intelligence led Him to invent the modern table. Theological qualms aside, the humor gives the audience a break, and at the same time, further fleshes out the portrait of Christ as a real man.

ENCOUNTER WITH CAIAPHAS

The Gospels make clear that Jesus had long been at odds with some of the more influential groups in first century Palestine, referred to in the New Testament as the Pharisees, the Elders, the Scribes, the Judeans (sometimes translated "the Jews"), and the High Priests. (The select group of seventy-one

39 Many people ask why Joseph, Mary's husband and Jesus' foster-father, an important member of the Holy Family and a key factor in the reality of Christ's normal human experience, doesn't appear in the film. The Gospels don't mention Joseph after the family trip to Jerusalem when Jesus was twelve years old. Christian tradition holds that Joseph died sometime between that trip and the beginning of Jesus' public ministry, eighteen years later.

leaders who served as the governing body for Israel at the time was called the Sanhedrin.) Jesus' doctrine and practices contradicted much of what the establishment considered true religion. His popularity was a potential threat to their authority and to the political aims they were pursuing with the Roman occupying forces. Less than a week before His arrest Jesus had entered Jerusalem riding a donkey to be greeted by throngs of followers and disciples who hailed Him as the promised King, the Son of David, and He hadn't contradicted them. (This triumphal entry is recalled in a later flashback, as Christ carries His cross through the streets of Jerusalem. Instead of the jeering, violent crowd watching Him physically struggle to walk, in the flashback the people honor Him with palm branches. Christians commemorate this event annually in the liturgy of Palm Sunday).

Some of these high-level enemies of Jesus undoubtedly believed they were defending the rights of God by trying to stop Him—after all, Jesus' claim of being divine was a capital crime of blasphemy in ancient Israel. The future St. Paul would have been one of these defenders of religious law. Others certainly believed they were preserving the very existence of their nation and way of life.[40] Maybe less noble motives were at work in others. Neither the Gospels nor the film go into the reasons,[41] both merely show these men as determined to do away with Jesus, to the point of being willing to falsify a trial and manipulate a low-life rabble.

40 John 11:47-53: The chief priests, therefore, and the Pharisees gathered a council and said: What do we, for this man doth many miracles? If we let him alone so, all will believe in him; and the Romans will come, and take away our place and nation. But one of them, named Caiphas, being the high priest that year, said to them: You know nothing. Neither do you consider that it is expedient for you that one man should die for the people and that the whole nation perish not. And this he spoke not of himself: but being the high priest of that year, he prophesied that Jesus should die for the nation. And not only for the nation, but to gather together in one the children of God that were dispersed. From that day therefore they devised to put him to death.

41 Matthew's Gospel, however, does mention that Pilate knew that for envy they [Caiphas and his accomplices] had delivered him [Jesus], (Matthew 27:18), and John records a conversation in which the leaders of Jerusalem conspired against Jesus. See previous footnote.

Later, the New Testament puts this opposition into the perspective of God's plan of redemption. When St. Peter is giving his first sermon to a crowd in Jerusalem he describes the death Jesus suffered at their hands, and then he adds: "And now, brethren, I know that you did it through ignorance, as did also your rulers. But those things which God before had shewed by the mouth of all the prophets, that his Christ should suffer, he hath so fulfilled."[42] St. Paul makes the same point in his first letter to the Christians in Corinth: "Which none of the princes of this world knew. For if they had known it, they would never have crucified the Lord of glory."[43] For this reason the Christian Church has always considered every sinner the author of Christ's death, not only those who were in Jerusalem on Good Friday.[44]

The film adds another very human angle to the motives of Jesus' persecutors, elaborating on the Gospel's mention of "envy"[45] as a key factor. Simply put, Jesus was upsetting the applecart. The leaders of Israel at this time were considerably corrupt. They hadn't always been like that, but it was a particularly bad moment for them in their history, and Jesus was threatening what they valued most: their power. People were listening to Jesus; His charisma was magnetic. He was healing the sick, He was teaching people things that made them feel better, that fed their souls. He was giving them the Beatitudes. So He incurred some of these leaders' rage and envy. Either they had to get Him out of the way, or else submit to Him. But pride blocked them from submitting. It's an unflatteringly human side of the Gospel story that the film faithfully alludes to.

42 Acts of the Apostles 3:17-18.

43 1 Corinthians 2:8.

44 Sinners were the authors and the ministers of all the sufferings that the divine Redeemer endured (Roman Catechism I, 5, 11).

45 Cf. Matthew 17:18.

The Gospels also refer to some Pharisees and Elders who were actually disciples of Jesus, men like Nicodemus and Joseph of Arimathea, who paid for Jesus' burial. In the months after Christ's Passion and Resurrection many of these high profile Jewish leaders changed their minds and joined the early Christian Church. The film brings this out by having these two members of the Sanhedrin come to Christ's defense during His appearance in front of Caiaphas and Annas, even though this is not documented in the biblical texts. The scene depicts the two members' objections to the trumped-up evidence and the unorthodox procedures being rudely silenced. Still, it lets the audience know that not all the residents of Jerusalem are enemies of Jesus.

On the other hand, the swift reaction to their protests as well as the guards' unchecked brutality against Jesus indicate that anyone who stood up for Jesus would suffer the consequences. This is a plausible explanation of why Jesus' supporters stayed in the background throughout the Passion—His followers were terrified for their own life. None of this is narrated by the Gospels, which only describe the Apostles' fear in the post-Resurrection passages[46] (though some details appear in Anne Catherine Emmerich's book). By making this allusion, the film accurately emphasizes the Christian doctrine that all sinners were the authors of Christ's Passion, not one particular race.

The Gospels actually record two trials, the first one in private with Annas, the former high priest and father-in-law to Caiaphas, who was then acting high priest and leader of the Sanhedrin. When Annas finishes with Jesus, he sends Him on to Caiaphas' courtyard, where He goes on trial before the Sanhedrin as a ruling body. To keep the drama and action moving in the

---

46 Cf. John 20:19.

film, the decision was made to only include one trial scene. Including every-thing about Jesus' Passion could easily lend itself to a four-hour film, albeit a grisly marathon. The final version is just over two hours. But it works. Still, after most of the early screenings, many viewers were clamoring to include more—more flashbacks, more Resurrection.

THE SILENCE OF A LAMB

Christ knows that He is innocent. He knows that He is being tried unjustly (according to the Sanhedrin's own rules, trials at night were considered invalid) and the accusations are false. He could have outwitted them in the courtroom just as He had confounded His enemies in many previous verbal battles. But He didn't. He remained curiously passive, virtually silent—ful-filling the prophets' predictions of the coming Redeemer. Just as lambs put up no resistance before they are slaughtered, so the suffering servant, the Messiah who was to redeem Israel, would quietly accept His victimhood: "He was offered because it was his own will, and he opened not his mouth; he shall be led as a sheep to the slaughter, and shall be dumb as a lamb before his shearer, and he shall not open his mouth."[47]

Why? He didn't have to defend Himself. He told the truth. It was all part of the divine plan. He knew when to stay silent, when to suffer the injustice, and when to defend Himself. A host of mysteries is presented here; not even the most astute theologians admit to having all the answers. In the Gospel accounts, Jesus did pepper His silence with certain comments at particular times. But why those comments, and why at those moments, and why so much silence?

Jesus Himself alludes to one of the reasons: He knew His accusers

47 Isaiah 53:7.

wouldn't listen. "If I shall tell you, you will not believe me. And if I shall also ask you, you will not answer me, nor let me go."[48] But He also knew that the Redeemer had to suffer in order to merit Redemption. He wouldn't defend Himself to the point of avoiding suffering, but only to the point of helping His persecutors see the truth of what they were doing. He had predicted His suffering to His Apostles three times, but they only understood after it was over:

> *The Son of man must suffer many things and be rejected by the ancients and chief priests and scribes and be killed and the third day rise again. … all things shall be accomplished which were written by the prophets concerning the Son of man. For he shall be delivered to the Gentiles and shall be mocked and scourged and spit upon, and after they have scourged him they will put him to death. And the third day he shall rise again.*[49]

Jesus foresaw it, every detail of it. Therefore, each of those details has a meaning, each is a strand in this story of faith, hope, love, and forgiveness.

---

48 Luke 22:67-68.

49 Luke 9:22; 18:31-33. Jesus made these predictions months before His Passion.

CHAPTER 4

TRIAL IN THE PRAETORIUM

WHAT'S ON PILATE'S MIND?

Palestine at the time of Jesus was neither an independent state nor a fully assimilated province within the Roman Empire. It had been subdued by the Romans in 33 B.C. but its political status had been in flux ever since, mostly due to the shrewd machinations of the Herodians, the family of rulers who had been governing Palestine since the first century B.C. The Herodians were half Jewish and half Idumean. When Rome subjected Palestine, they were Rome's natural (and willing) choice as deputy. The Herodian line of rulers acted as mediator between the Roman and the Jewish authorities, all the while seeking their own aggrandizement.

It was a dangerous game, because many of Palestine's Jewish communities were fiercely independent, ready to disturb the peace in order to further their cause. At the same time the Romans had one goal: order. To keep their power, therefore, the Herodians walked a delicate line. They had to convince the locals that they were in favor of Jewish independence and simultaneously make the Romans believe they were fostering Palestine's assimilation into the Roman Empire.

The Herodians ended up satisfying no one except the Herodians. Following the death of Herod the Great (soon after Jesus' birth in Bethlehem), Rome sent a Procurator to keep a closer watch on Palestine. Even so, rebellions occasionally broke out, and anti-Roman sentiments were on the rise throughout Christ's lifetime. One political party, called the Zealots, was dedicated exclusively to establishing independence at any cost. The situation became so troublesome that in A.D. 70 Rome finally sent an army to raze Jerusalem and scatter the Judeans throughout the Empire. That occurred forty years after Jesus was crucified, but it illustrates the volatile relationship existing between Rome, the Herodian dynasty, and the Jewish leaders—a significant factor in the events that led to Jesus' death.

Whoever had the position of Procurator, therefore, was in a political conundrum. He couldn't satisfy the local inhabitants without granting concessions towards independence, but doing so would antagonize his superiors back in Rome. Since it was an outlying province, the best the Roman appointee could hope for was to establish a modicum of stability. If he maintained order long enough, there might be a promotion in his future—to somewhere where he could advance his career while breathing a bit more easily. If he failed, he might find himself shipped off to a more remote location, farther from Rome.

Pontius Pilate was the Roman Procurator at the time of Christ's Passion. He had already violently put down a pair of small rebellions, and had received warnings from the Emperor about keeping things in order. An ambitious and worldly man (who also seems to have been highly superstitious), he was keenly aware of the delicacy of his position. The film brings this out in Pilate's conversations with Claudia Procles, his wife, conversations that do not appear in the Gospels. It also is evident the first time the Roman guards see Jesus being dragged into court and smell trouble brewing; they don't hesitate to send a message to Abenader, Pilate's right-hand man.

The historical intricacies of Palestine's political situation that the Gospels only obliquely acknowledge (by recording that Christ's trial gave Pilate and Herod a chance to become friends) add to the gripping realism of the film. Pilate was a man already in trouble with Caesar. His job security was precarious. Mixed with his tendency to superstition and vulnerability for portents and astrology (characteristics attested to by contemporary writers), made for an unstable combination. That epitomizes Pilate. He didn't know which way to go. He was getting too many signals, wrong ones, right ones, conscience, ambition, fear. The film has no qualms about asserting that the Devil was in the mix too, trying to drag Pilate one way while he was being torn the other way by his wife's dreams. He was a real man struggling with a real decision, and in the end he caved in. On the inside, he was simply weak.

THE AUTHORITY TO KILL

According to the Jewish law of the time, the just punishment for blasphemy —the crime Jesus had been convicted of—was death. The Jewish leaders, however, lacked the authority to administer the death penalty; the Romans had usurped that authority to further their plan of conquest and assimilation. As a result, Caiaphas and his accomplices had to bring Jesus before the Roman Procurator and convince him to ratify the death sentence. They knew it would be tricky, for two reasons.

First, Pilate had little respect for Jewish laws and customs, as he had already demonstrated more than once during his tour of duty there. The Romans tended to stay aloof from their subjects' religious practices, though they were tolerant as long as the practices didn't interfere with the mandatory worship of the State gods. Getting embroiled in religious disputes with "the natives" would likely be unappetizing for Pilate.

Second, Caiaphas and his contingent of leaders knew that Pilate would be well aware of Jesus' popularity. His triumphant entry into Jerusalem amid adoring crowds hailing Him as the Messiah, the Son of David, and the promised King of Israel would hardly have gone unnoticed by this astute politician. How was Pilate to know that the same crowds who hailed Jesus as their Messiah five days earlier wouldn't react violently against the Procurator's handing out a death sentence? Hindsight shows the unlikelihood of such an eventuality, but Pilate didn't have the luxury of hindsight.

MORE THAN MERE POLITICS

The repartee between Caiaphas, Annas, and Pilate brings these issues to light, and understanding the background helps clarify the subtext of those exchanges. But Christian tradition sees a deeper meaning behind the mundane political reality.

One of the differences between God's Old Covenant and Jesus' New Covenant is the idea of universality. The New Covenant, so Christians believe, extends the favor God had shown to a single nation in the Old Covenant (the Chosen People of Israel) to the entire human family (the "Gentile nations" as the Old Testament refers to non-Israelites). This idea appears frequently throughout the New Testament. After His Resurrection, Jesus sends His Apostles on a mission to the whole world: "Going therefore, teach ye all nations: baptizing them in the name of the Father and of the Son and of the Holy Ghost. Teaching them to observe all things whatsoever I have commanded you. And behold I am with you all days, even to the consummation of the world."[50] St. Paul repeatedly expresses the universality of Christ's redemption by applying it to both Jews and Greeks ("Greeks" was a catch-all term for non-Jews, since Greek was the common language spoken by the different peoples who comprised the eastern Empire): "There is neither Jew nor Greek, there is neither bond nor free, there is neither male nor female. For

50 Matthew 28:19-20.

you are all one in Christ Jesus."[51]

The frequent cropping up of heretical and schismatic factions in the early Christian Church often threatened this universality. By the second century, the bishops who remained faithful to the doctrine of Christ's Apostles were using the term "catholic" (from the Greek word for "universal") to distinguish between those divisive factions and the many authentic Christian communities. This was the origin of the name, "The Catholic Church."

For Christ's self-sacrifice to have such universal repercussions, it would have to be offered in a universal context, under the condemnation not only of Caiaphas and other Jewish leaders, but also with the approval of the Gentile leaders, represented by Pilate. Since "one died for all,"[52] since the Savior takes upon Himself the responsibility for the sins of all, it is appropriate that all nations, all peoples are implicated in His suffering and death. As a result, the salvation purchased by that suffering and death is offered to all peoples, not only to Israel. "For the grace of God our Savior hath appeared to all men," St. Paul writes in his New Testament letter to Titus.[53]

Since God is all-powerful and all-knowing, He could have chosen to send the Savior at a different moment of history, one when Israel was independent, for instance. But He didn't. From a Christian perspective, the involvement of the Roman government in Christ's Passion and death is no accident, just as it was no accident that Jesus was born in Bethlehem instead of Joseph and Mary's hometown of Nazareth. In that case as well, God's plan of salvation mysteriously moved forward through the mediation of a mundane governmental reality: a decree requiring all families to travel back to their

51 Galatians 3:28.

52 2 Corinthians 5:14.

53 Titus 2:11.

tribal city so Caesar could take an imperial census.

Authentic Christian spirituality always includes this incarnational, i.e. concrete and historical, dimension. For Christians, God's omnipotence doesn't show itself in His forceful domination of human freedom. Rather, it is revealed in His marvelous orchestration of a divine plan of salvation in and through the flesh-and-blood realities of the human condition, human freedom included. As St. Theresa of Avila expressed it in the 1500s: "I find God amidst the pots and pans."

CLAUDIA PROCLES: PILATE'S WIFE AND ANGEL

Pilate's reluctance to have Jesus executed stemmed from more than merely political motives. His wife had had a harrowing dream about Jesus the night before. It stirred up Pilate's own reservations about ratifying the death sentence. Though the film elaborated on the exchanges between Pilate and Claudia, their factualness springs right from the Gospels: "And as he [Pilate] was sitting in the place of judgment, his wife sent to him, saying 'Have thou nothing to do with that just man, for I have suffered many things this day in a dream because of him.'"[54]

Many spiritual writers have been fascinated by this biblical reference to Claudia's dream. It moved her to interrupt and interfere with state affairs while they were taking place. It must have been an uncannily vivid, specific dream. It is commonly seen as a prompting of the Holy Spirit, a way to give Pilate a chance against the powers of evil.

Throughout this sequence, Pilate's indecision and frustration emerge. He is a seething bundle of contradictory desires, trying desperately to please everyone in order to save his own status and career. Sending Jesus to be

[54] Matthew 27:19.

judged by Herod was his first escape ploy. When that didn't work Pilate
played the governor's amnesty card—using his authority to free one criminal
on the Jewish Passover (an annual tradition used by the Romans). *Certainly,*
Pilate thought, *the people will choose to free the condemned rabbi.*

And yet, Christ's suffering and death was, from the Gospels' perspective, preordained. Was Pilate really free to decide in Jesus' favor? Wasn't He
the victim of destiny?

The film offers no easy answer, which makes Pilate come across as
so believable. The ambiguity and tension surrounding his character elicit
compassion. Pilate's struggle is everyman's struggle: the clash of two deeply
human instincts, one that longs to adhere to truth, and another that grasps
at mere expediency. Christian doctrine on human freedom (which asserts
that God doesn't violate that freedom) implies that Pilate could have done
the right thing (though theologians can only surmise how it all would have
worked out). Claudia's dream implies that God wanted him to do it. Yet the
truth remains: in the end every person has to make choices. God *knows* the
future, but He doesn't *determine* the future. It's a thorny theological distinc-
tion, but Pilate's anxiety shows how true it really is.

DID JESUS SPEAK LATIN?

The conversations between Jesus and Pilate follow the Gospel narratives,
but the film depicts them in a fresh way that emphasizes this unique verbal
exchange. During both conversations Jesus looks pitiful. Beaten, chained, and
bleeding (much more so in the conversation that takes place after His flagellation), He is the epitome of weakness. But even in that condition, He is the
one in charge. The first stage direction after Pilate has taken Jesus inside the
Praetorium (the residence of the Procurator) and offered Him a drink makes
it clear. The screenplay reads, "Jesus lifts his eyes to Pilate. He ignores the

wine, but holds the Roman's eyes in his. Pilate studies the torn clothes, the blood-encrusted neck, feet and hands of Jesus."

Pilate is nervous, pacing and fidgeting, unable to meet Jesus' strong and purposeful gaze. Everything Jesus says seems aimed not at defending Himself, but at goading Pilate toward the right decision. He rebuts Pilate's first question with a question of His own, taking the high ground and forcing Pilate to face his own conscience. Jesus brings up the issue of truth, but He doesn't give an easy answer when Pilate lashes out, "Truth? What is truth?" He looks straight at the Roman (the screenplay describes the look: "Jesus does not answer. His eyes pierce Pilate's."). Pilate is staring Truth in the face, but will he believe? Will he make an act of faith?

Pilate begins this conversation speaking Aramaic, the native language of Palestine at the time. Jesus answers him in Latin. Some biblical scholars who screened early versions of the film found this hard to swallow. Most accepted the decision to have Pilate speaking Aramaic, albeit grudgingly, since Greek was the more common international language at the time. But to have Jesus speaking Latin went outside the parameters of many scholars, despite the fact that some of the most recent scholarship depicts Galilee as a place where Latin was frequently spoken. Common sense, however, supplies more than a few justifications of the language choice. Palestine had been crawling with Romans for decades, and Galilee, where Jesus grew up, was a market region where all the major languages were used. He was a handyman whose skills were sought by diverse consumers from different parts of the world—including, probably, more than a few Latin-speakers. Simply discounting the possibility, therefore, seems arbitrary.

That answers how Jesus could have known Latin, but it doesn't answer why the film chooses to have Him speaking Latin. The reason was simple: Jesus wanted to make sure Pilate fully understood Him. Pilate knows Aramaic, but it's not his mother tongue. If Jesus addresses him in Latin, there is no communication problem. The screenplay shows Jesus meeting Pilate on his terms, speaking his language.

Jesus is more interested in saving Pilate's moral integrity, saving him from betraying his conscience, than defending His own innocence. He could have unleashed His divine authority, made Pilate cower in fear, forcing him to do right, but He didn't. He met Pilate right where he was, opening the door of truth and inviting him to come through it. This kindness of a tortured, condemned man towards His unjust judge comes across again in the second conversation, where Pilate and Jesus stand side-by-side above the screaming crowd. Once again Pilate is desperately looking for an easy way out, yet Jesus gently invites him to take the hard road, because it's the right road.

Scholars may disagree about whether Jesus and Pilate really conversed in Latin, but they can't disagree with the possible reasons behind it. If God went to the trouble of becoming a man so He could speak face to face with sinners, you can be sure that He will do everything possible to make the truth of Himself and His message understandable to anyone He encounters. It's a great source of hope for all people in search of life's meaning. Hearing and heeding that truth, however, as Pilate's response shows, depends on more than grammar and syntax.

FROM JESUS' POINT OF VIEW

Two moments during Jesus' appearance before Pilate deserve special comment. When Jesus first arrives in the courtyard below Pilate's throne of judgment (while His enemies are provoking the crowd for His destruction), He looks up into the sky and sees a white dove.

This detail wasn't in the screenplay. It occurred to Jim Caviezel while they were filming. "It's such a horrible thing—the trials, the injustice, the beating.… I just thought that through it all Jesus keeps up His hope, and it seemed like His seeing that dove would show that. " Jim Caviezel is familiar with the symbolism of the dove, which stands for peace in the Old Testament and for the Holy Spirit in the New Testament. "It's like a sign from the Father, a reminder that His Father's hand is still holding Him." The glimpse of the dove, a sign of the Father's solicitude, calls to mind a phrase from one of the Bible's most well known passages: "The Lord ruleth me, and I shall want nothing.… For though I should walk in the midst of the shadow of death, I will fear no evils, for thou art with me. Thy rod and thy staff, they have comforted me."[55] Fewer valleys could be as dark as the one Jesus was walking through during His Passion. Seeing God's peace hovering above Him drives home the lesson of hope, one of the key themes of the movie.[56]

The second moment occurs when Pilate offers the crowd a choice between freeing Barabbas or freeing Jesus. Close-ups of the two condemned men leave no doubt about who deserves pardon. When Barabbas is chosen, Pilate reluctantly releases him. The camera immediately focuses on Jesus, who seems to gasp in disappointment. Did He really think He might be set free? Hadn't He already accepted His Passion back in Gethsemane? Was He wavering when the possibility of pardon appeared?

Jim Caviezel was trying to keep two opposing sentiments in play at that moment, as well as throughout the film. "On the one hand He's God, so He knows everything. But how can you act that out? He was also a real man. And any real man would have felt horror at that time. I had to show that."

55 Psalm 22:1,4.

56 It also echoes another line from the Psalms that expresses a man's hope in the midst of severe difficulties: And I said, Who will give me wings like a dove, and I will fly and be at rest? (Psalm 54:7).

It clearly isn't a merely human disappointment. We see Jesus' face again, in another close-up, as Barabbas makes his way down the stairs. It exhibits no resentment or anxiety. Jesus simply looks deeply into Barabbas' eyes, disconcerting him. Once again Jesus is interested more in drawing a lost soul into His heart than saving His own life.

Others interpret the gasp of disappointment differently from Jim Caviezel. They link it to the people who were making that awful decision. They were frenzied and fell victim to a mob mentality, which they would regret later on, as Jesus knew. So Jesus felt sorry for them, not for Himself. A similar moment occurs later, after the flagellation, when Pilate tells Jesus, "Don't you realize I have the power to crucify you?" Jesus replies, "You'd have no power over me if it weren't given you from above, but it is he who delivered me to you that has the greater sin. " When Jim says that line a tear trickles down his cheek. Jesus is deeply saddened by this new betrayal, but the sadness stems from His disappointment in the crowd; He's thinking about them.

Great art can encompass multilayered interpretations. In either case, whether for Jim's reason or others, what comes out is Christ's humanity. The decisions of His fellow human beings—for good or for ill—don't leave Him indifferent.

CHAPTER 5

✠

TRIAL IN HEROD'S PALACE

If Pilate typifies the man of affairs, trudging forward under the merciless whip of worldly ambition, Herod is the quintessence of sensuality.

When Rome had established the procuratorship, it divided Palestine into four zones (the Tetrarchy), some of which were put under the governorship of the Herodians. At the time of Christ's Passion, Galilee, the region where Jesus grew up and spent most of His last three years, was ruled by Herod Antipas. Herod married his sister-in-law, Herodias, and sent John the Baptist, Jesus' relative, to his death.

In the film Herod comes across as extremely effeminate and pleasure-loving. It is an interesting choice, considering that Herod was a man accustomed to wielding power easily and ruthlessly. Herod was someone used to getting whatever he wanted. His moral strength had been sapped by a life of unbridled self-indulgence, an extreme "rich-kid" syndrome. Herod's world was completely decadent.

HEROD'S STORY

The Gospels portray that same dimension of Herod, especially when he caves in to his wife's bloodthirsty demand for John the Baptist's head. John the Baptist was the last and greatest of the prophets. He announced the presence of the Savior and called the people of Israel to repentance. John also denounced Herod for marrying his sister-in-law, Herodias (she seems to have seduced him, thinking that he offered a better climb up the social ladder than his brother, Philip the Tetrarch), an incestuous crime for the Jews of the time. Herod had the outspoken prophet arrested and imprisoned.

The Gospels say Herod refused to execute John (it was Herodias who was anxious to do away with the bothersome soothsayer) because he was afraid of causing an uproar among the people, who revered the prophet. There was also something about his conversations with John that moved him: "… For Herod feared John, knowing him to be a just and holy man, and kept him, and when he heard him, did many things, and he heard him willingly."[57]

Herod finally gave in to Herodias' insistent pressure. The Gospels paint a vivid picture of the tragedy:

> *And when a convenient day was come, Herod made a supper for his birthday, for the princes, and tribunes, and chief men of Galilee. And when the daughter of the same Herodias had come in, and had danced, and pleased Herod, and them that were at table with him, the king said to the damsel: Ask of me what thou wilt, and I will give it thee. And he swore to her: Whatsoever thou shalt ask I will give thee, though it be the half of my kingdom. Who when she was gone out, said to her mother,*

57 Mark 6:20.

What shall I ask? But her mother said: The head of John the Baptist.
And when she was come in immediately with haste to the king, she asked,
saying: I will that forthwith thou give me in a dish, the head of John the
Baptist. And the king was struck sad. Yet because of his oath, and because
of them that were with him at table, he would not displease her: But
sending an executioner, he commanded that his head should be brought
in a dish. And he beheaded him in the prison, and brought his head in a
dish: and gave it to the damsel, and the damsel gave it her mother.[58]

The Gospels add one other insight into Herod's personality: he had long wanted to meet Jesus because he hoped to see Him perform some fantastic miracle.[59] Herod's interest in religion was, at best, superficial.

JESUS, HEROD, AND PILATE: CONTRASTING WAYS OF LIFE

When Jesus went before Pilate, He was willing to speak, because He saw in Pilate a glimmer of honor. With Herod, Jesus stays utterly silent. He knows that a lifetime of extravagant self-indulgence has all but extinguished Herod's capacity to see any further than his reputation, his comfort zone, and his sensual pleasures. Jesus always performed His miracles in response to the faith of men and women who knew their need for God and put their trust in Him, not for sheer entertainment.

But even in the midst of decadence, once again, the film offers a moment of hope. Jesus connects to one sensitive soul. Looking at one of the slaves, Jesus catches his eye; the slave averts His look, ashamed. It's the only point of human contact in the scene. This visual encounter doesn't appear in the screenplay; it was added during the shooting, using one of the production

58 Mark 6:21-28.

59 Luke 23:8.

team members for the role instead of an actor. It is the man's face that makes the moment work, because he has a look of such innocence and serenity, the exact opposite of everything Herod stands for.

Pilate and Herod, both tragic and unforgettable figures in the Gospels as well as the film, exhibit the emptiness of a life that lacks faith, hope, and love. They are too wrapped up in their self-centeredness to recognize God's presence in their lives. They paid more attention to their idols of worldly success and pleasure than they did to the demands of truth and justice. Christ's love was unable to penetrate their hearts.

The film makes you feel these two moral disasters more than it makes you understand them. The visual contrast between Christ and His judges evokes the feeling even more than the dialogues. Jesus—chained, beaten, and humiliated—is the embodiment of both physical pain and societal failure, the very realities that Herod and Pilate have spent their lives avoiding. Herod is draped in silk robes and surrounded by luxury; Pilate wears the distinguished garb of political office and military prowess. Herod is physically soft and languid in both body and voice; Pilate is virile and strong. Christ stands before each man, an icon of self-sacrifice, giving up everything for the sake of true justice, fulfilling God's plan of salvation out of love for His fellow men. He is a silent reproach to both of His judges.

And yet, Jesus doesn't condemn them, doesn't give them the slightest look of scorn. He endures their rejection, their petty egoism; He neither judges them, nor rejects them. His patient endurance seems to express a hidden hope that they will take a step toward Him. The viewer is left with a sense that Christ would have responded to the smallest act of humility with a flood of grace and light. In that sense, Christ's hope spreads hope in those who watch Him. As they too see Herod and Pilate—and perhaps themselves—they react with compassion, not just reproof.

COUNTERPOINT

Claudia Procles, Pilate's wife, is the perfect counterpoint. She heeds the voice in her heart that proclaims Christ's innocence and goodness. Though she can do nothing directly to halt the injustice, she does everything she can indirectly. When Pilate gives in to Caiaphas' and the crowd's demands and sentences Jesus to death, the film shows Claudia's disappointment as she turns from the window and walks slowly back into the palace. Though she is heartbroken, she is at peace. She did all that was in her power to defend the truth; she didn't lose faith. Pilate, on the other hand, remains ill at ease, even after making his decision. The final onscreen image of Pilate is from a distance as he watches Christ carrying His cross to Calvary. There is no mistaking the ambivalence, the lingering doubt in Pilate's face. Christ's official trial is over, but Pilate's inner trial rages on.[60]

MARY AND THE DIGNITY OF LOVE

Why was Claudia able to see the truth and keep her faith while Pilate was not? Would she have been less interested than her husband in Pilate's career, in their future, their reputation, and their comfort? It's the mystery of human freedom once again, just as it had appeared in the contrast between Judas and Peter. But in Claudia's case, the film adds another ingredient.

Claudia is following the trial in the Praetorium from a high window. From her vantage point, she is able to see Pilate, Jesus, and the crowd. She also notices Mary, Jesus' mother, when she enters the courtyard with John and Magdalene. She not only notices Mary; she is moved by seeing

---

60 Many critics accuse the film of portraying Pilate in a positive light and Caiaphas in a negative light. This criticism reflects more about the critics than about the film. Clearly, Pilate is a tragic figure, as is Caiaphas. Both do the wrong thing. If Pilate appears more sympathetic, it is only because it is easier for people today to identify with his lack of moral conviction. He has no moral convictions that give him spiritual strength; he is wishy-washy, trying to please everyone and climb the ladder of success. Caiaphas, on the other hand, has deep moral convictions; he doesn't doubt himself; he knows what he believes in. That, for good or for ill, is an unpopular posture in postmodern society.

her. Something about Mary catches her attention. The screenplay is more explicit: "It is [Mary's] dignity that catches Claudia's attention.... Claudia studies Mary and her two companions with interest."

Claudia follows the trial not only through Pilate's eyes, not only through Jesus' eyes, but also through Mary's eyes. The artistic choice indicates that Claudia drew some of her strength and determination, some of her faith and hope in the power of the truth, from Mary. It is more than an artistic choice, however; it is the constant experience of Christians throughout the two millennia of Christian history. Remaining close to the faithful, loving Mother is the best way to insure one's own loving fidelity to the Son. The earliest Christian works of art (preserved in the Roman catacombs) depict Jesus with His mother Mary; one of the earliest non-biblical Christian prayers is a petition for Mary's motherly assistance amid the difficulties of Christian discipleship.[61] One can't help but wonder whether Pilate might have made the right choice if he, like Claudia, had seen Mary, firm and faithful, amidst the furious crowd.

---

61 The *sub tuum praesidium:* We turn to you for protection, holy Mother of God. Listen to our prayers and help us in our needs. Save us from every danger, glorious and blessed Virgin.

CHAPTER 6

＊✝＊

THE FLAGELLATION

Flagellation, also called flogging or scourging, was a common punishment for criminals and slaves in the ancient world. Sometimes it was even a form of execution, as some of the tools used (the ones eyed greedily by the film's Roman guards when they were told to change instruments) make clear. The screenplay also delineates this when Pilate gives the order: "See to it that the punishment is severe, Abenader, but do not let them kill the man." Sometimes flagellation was used to weaken criminals before they were executed. In the case of Jesus, Pilate was hoping that it would satisfy Caiaphas and free himself from having to ratify or deny the death sentence.

The method of scourging depicted in the movie reflects most historical studies. First the criminal would be bruised with rods, his skin would be broken open with a whip, then his flesh would be torn with a whip tipped with sharp pieces of bone or metal. Experts disagree on some of the details, but are unanimous on the appalling severity of the punishment.

Because the methods were so brutal, and the penalty so common, the men assigned the task of punishing and executing criminals were usually hardened soldiers, if not criminals themselves. Compassion wasn't called for in the job description.

TOO GRAPHIC?

Even knowing all this, the overriding sentiment when one witnesses this brutal sequence is disbelief. It couldn't have been that horrible, could it?

Early on in the production process, critics launched an accusation of gratuitous violence against the film, responding to rumors of the extremely graphic depiction of the flagellation and crucifixion. But much thought and research went into this particular aspect. In other film versions of Jesus' life, death, and resurrection, the failure to show the real physical brutality that He suffered is one of the things that is unsatisfying for many moviegoers. This film doesn't show the full reality either, at least if you accept what the mystics and visionaries say about it. Most historians agree with them on that point. The consultants for this film investigated the historical record: how Roman prisoners at the time were treated, what flagellation "looked" like, how crucifixion worked. They also examined multiple studies of the Shroud of Turin,[62] which shows an entire body lacerated by more than a hundred lashings, far beyond the Deuteronomic limit of forty. The Shroud shows that welts from the flagellation covered Jesus' body, blood drenched His head and face, and holes were driven right through his hands. The film attempts to make this as real and accurate as possible, while toning it down just enough for the audience to actually watch it.

But was it really necessary to show so much violence? Wouldn't a taste of it been enough? From a Christian perspective, none of the violence is

---

62 An ancient linen cloth preserved in the Cathedral of Turin, Italy, reputed to be the actual burial shroud of Jesus.

gratuitous. The purpose is not to make viewers squirm and say, "How gross!" It's there because that's what Jesus suffered. Those are the wounds that heal. It really happened, and so, the film seems to say, if God let it happen, there must be a reason for it.

What is the reason? Few would claim to understand all the theological ins and outs of it, but you can't really tell the story right without showing what really happened. Christian doctrine teaches that God suffered for every human being, that He freely chose to endure extreme physical violence for the salvation of sinners. What does such a decision indicate? The fact that someone would willingly take on such excessive torment demonstrates an extreme intensity of love—God's love.

That's why the film has to go there. Jesus chose a hard and excessive price of salvation. One of the reasons other Passion films don't elicit the same kind of visceral reaction is because they don't make you face the enormity of that sacrifice.

Every stroke of the cane and the whip constitutes one more rejection of Jesus Christ, who, Christians believe, is the incarnation of God's love. Every stroke of the cane and the whip symbolizes a rejection of God's love. Rejecting God's love, turning away from His loving plan, is the essence of sin. Each stroke, therefore, stands for a sin. Because Jesus took upon Himself all of mankind's sins, He is taking on more sins than any one person can imagine—this is the theological implication of the "excessive" torment the film attempts to depict. The sufferings of the Savior needed to be in proportion to the sins of those He came to save.

MULTIFARIOUS REACTIONS

Jim Caviezel adds another insight. He remembers seeing the film *Saving*

Private Ryan in a theater full of teenagers. A group of rambunctious teens near the front were cheering noisily during the opening scene on the beach, a graphic scene filled with harrowing images of massacre and human carnage. "Some people just get a kick out of violence, as if their heart has been deadened," Jim says. "The difference in *The Passion* is that they see not only the violence, but they also see people like themselves inflicting it up on the screen—the brutal guards. Maybe it will be a chance for them to get a better look at themselves."

Jim noticed a similar reaction among some workers on the set when he would walk from the make-up trailer to the soundstage in full bloody costume. "The whole time we were filming there would be three kinds of reactions when people saw me—I mean, they did an incredible job of making me look just like Jesus, and people would really react. The first reaction was indifference. Some people just don't care about Jesus; he doesn't move them or interest them in the least. Others laughed; they thought it was funny, and fun to have a scourged guy walking around. Others felt compassion; they would come up to me and say things, or hug me. Some even asked me to bless them. I think the real Jesus Christ faced all three of these reactions. And they all show up in the film. I think that's going to make a difference. When people see their own reaction to Jesus depicted on the film it might shock them, it might make them think."

The early screenings seemed to prove him right. One woman, a devout, practicing Catholic Christian, was sorely tempted to leave the screening room during the flagellation scene. But as she was getting up, a thought occurred to her: "If he actually *endured* that out of love for me, the least I can do in return is to endure *watching* it."

THE GUARDS' EXAGGERATED CRUELTY

Those explanations may make psychological and theological sense, but an audience needs a realistic hook to hang on to. The film provides it in the cruel soldiers, border guards, whose job was torture and execution. These were men who spent their time punishing criminals and massacring rebels. Their lives were miserable; they didn't like being where they were; they didn't like doing what they were doing. Consciously or unconsciously, they took out their frustrations on someone else. In short, they were thugs.

To emphasize this, during the filming they were given some lines made up on the spur of the moment. The translations don't appear in the subtitles, but they say things like "He's not a king, he's a magician.... Write me a poem on his back.... I'll write it in blood.... I'll make music, happy music...." The guards are also shown drinking. On a merely human level it helps explain their extreme brutality and revolting jocosity. Again, this was an element drawn from the meditations of Anne Catherine Emmerich, who envisioned the guards and soldiers becoming more and more inebriated, starting with the flagellation and continuing all the way to the crucifixion.

Other techniques also went into making the horrible violence tolerable. It had to be real and believable, but dramatically it had to be syncopated. It was critical for the film to offer escape hatches, visual images that could counterbalance the physical violence. Critics point to the onscreen time of the flagellation scene to back up their accusations of gratuitous violence. In actuality, the added length results from these moments of relief, not from the torture itself.

The camera moves to Mary while she's walking in the portico, to Claudia Procles, to Magdalene and John. Then it shifts back to Mary again, and to the Devil, and to the other characters. Flashbacks are effectively used.

These other images come and assail the audience, almost lyrically, giving the imagination a respite from the horrific violence. Even so, this part of the film does push you over the edge to drive home the gravity of the suffering. That's how it happened, and it happened that way for a reason.

ANOTHER GLIMPSE INTO JESUS' HEART

As the flagellation is about to begin, you see Jesus chained to the marble stump, shaking with fearful anticipation reminiscent of His combat in Gethsemane. As in Gethsemane, He utters a prayer: "My heart is ready, O God, my heart is ready."[63] This too is a line from the Psalms, just like His prayer in Gethsemane. The Gospels make no mention of Christ praying during the flagellation. Co-screenwriter Benedict Fitzgerald chose to put that line there, drawing on insights from Peter Gallwey's *The Watches of the Passion*.[64] He explains why: "The Psalms were the prayers that Jesus used his whole life—all the people of Israel used them. They too are inspired by God, and they reflect the complexity of the human spirit more effectively even than poetry. Certainly something was going on in Jesus' mind and heart while he suffered; the Psalms were our best guess at exactly what. We felt confident in the choice because the Gospel does have Jesus praying a Psalm later on, while he is dying on the cross."

Those who are familiar with the Psalms will appreciate the richness of the allusion. The Psalms are well known in Christian spirituality as the "school of trust in God," the place where the believer goes to rehabilitate the trust that original sin fractured. As a result, the Psalms often put expressions of distress and helplessness back-to-back with shouts of joy and confidence in God's goodness. This incongruous mix embodies the truth of human

63 Psalm 56:8.

64 See appendix for a biography of Peter Gallwey.

prayer, because that is the truth of the human condition: God meets man where man dwells, in a world shattered by suffering, confusion, and injustice. Precisely there God teaches the human heart to believe, to hope, and to love.

Christ's brief prayer and look heavenwards as He braces Himself for the scourging express—and teach—all of that. Here is the whole text of the Psalm from which Jesus' prayer is taken. It reveals the faith, hope, and love surging through Christ's heart as the forces of evil tear at His flesh (in Christ's prayer, the enemies the Psalm refers to would not be primarily the men who are punishing Him—He has come to save them—but the Ancient Enemy, the Devil, Satan, the instigator of evil and of the Fall, whose kingdom of sin was destroyed by the unconquerable love exhibited throughout Christ's Passion). As you read it, imagine Christ praying it in His heart while He is being brought to the flagellation courtyard—it perfectly expresses His deep anguish and His unshakable confidence in God:

> *Have mercy on me, O God, have mercy on me: for my soul trusteth in*
> *thee. And in the shadow of thy wings will I hope,*
> *until iniquity pass away.*
> *I will cry to God the most High;*
> *to God who hath done good to me.*
> *He hath sent from heaven and delivered me:*
> *he hath made them a reproach that trod upon me.*
> *God hath sent his mercy and his truth,*
> *and he hath delivered my soul from the midst of the young lions.*
> *I slept troubled.*
> *The sons of men,*
> *whose teeth are weapons and arrows,*
> *and their tongue a sharp sword.*
> *Be thou exalted, O God, above the heavens,*

and thy glory above all the earth.

They prepared a snare for my feet;

and they bowed down my soul.

They dug a pit before my face, and they are fallen into it.

My heart is ready, O God, my heart is ready:

I will sing, and rehearse a psalm.

Arise, O my glory, arise psaltery and harp:

I will arise early.

I will give praise to thee, O Lord, among the people:

I will sing a psalm to thee among the nations.

For thy mercy is magnified even to the heavens:

and thy truth unto the clouds.

Be thou exalted, O God, above the heavens:

and thy glory above all the earth.[65]

THE DEVIL'S HEYDAY

Satan makes a couple of appearances during the flagellation, gliding unobtrusively through the onlookers and the soldiers, smiling slightly, pleased, seemingly egging on the evil spectacle. It's as if the Devil shows up to make sure things are going according to plan. The whole Passion was, as the Gospels record, the Devil's hour, his chance to take his best shot at the Savior, to make Him reject God's will and follow in Adam's footsteps.

Originally, the screenplay envisioned showing more of Satan. There was discussion to include multiple demons, whispering in the ears of the crowd during the trial, and directly choreographing the brutality of the guards as they scourge Jesus. The filmmakers opted out of so blatant a satanic presence, not for theological reasons, but for artistic ones. The image just

65 Psalm 56:2-12.

didn't work. The goal was to keep everything as real as possible. The film had to show that the Devil was involved, because he was; but it had to avoid overdoing it so that it becomes hokey.

When they began screening the initial version, even this reduced presence of Satan received mixed reactions. Some people were especially turned off by the demonic baby in Satan's arms. One viewer called it "creepy. And the Gospel is not creepy."

For a while, the editors considered cutting that image, but in the end they made a conscious decision to keep it. Certain people might think: *That's weird, we don't get that.* It certainly is a little weird; it's more than a little weird. It's a picture of motherhood. When you first see the figure in the crowd, the first thought is, *There's a mother and a child, there's a little sign of hope maybe.* Then the child turns around, and it's all wrong! It's disturbing. It reiterates the idea of evil that runs as a motif throughout the film: evil as a distortion of something good. What's more tender and beautiful than a mother and her child? Satan takes that and distorts it—an androgynous figure holding a forty-year old "baby" with hair on his back. It is weird, it is shocking.

That's the theological reason behind Satan's baby, but it serves an artistic purpose as well. The torture is getting worse at that moment. The guards turn Jesus over to scourge Him on His chest. Seeing the Devil is a distraction. You need that distraction from the violence, but it must be different. It can't be just the same figure coming back over and over again. You notice a difference, she's holding something, but you don't know what it is at first, so the image draws you away from the beating, giving your imagination somewhere else to go.

Testament, Christ identifies Himself with every human being, and teaches His disciples that whatever they do or fail to do for their neighbor, they do or fail to do for Him. It is a logical application of the two great commandments of the Old Covenant, which Jesus bound together as one: "Thou shalt love the Lord thy God with thy whole heart.... Thou shalt love thy neighbor as thyself."[66] Jesus even explains that each person will be judged on how effectively they loved those neighbors who were in need. Claudia, merely from watching Jesus and Mary, learned this lesson and put it into practice. She couldn't do a whole lot to alleviate their pain, but what she could do, she did.

A TRIO OF GRIEF

Of Jesus' three faithful followers, only John can hold back his tears during the flagellation. He stands strong, his endurance buoying up, to some extent, Mary and Magdalene amidst their affliction. When they momentarily recover, however, and begin to wipe up the pools of Jesus' blood with the white linens, John breaks down.

This emotional give and take between John, Mary, and Magdalene was an artistic winner. From the beginning of the film, the challenge for the filmmakers was to sustain the grief of Jesus' followers through the whole film. How many ways are there to show misery? The film plays this trio of characters to make it work. When one of them loses composure, another doesn't; when one gets exhausted, another gives support. They journey together. In this interplay, the trio becomes an icon of the Christian community, accompanying Jesus along His path of sorrow, linked by their love for the Lord, and expressing that love in their support for each other.

66 Cf. Matthew 22:37-39.

JESUS' FLASHBACK: THE BLOODSTAINED SANDAL
AND THE WASHING OF THE FEET

Before the guards drag Jesus away from the flagellation loggia, He has another flashback. When they turn Him over to whip His chest, the camera zeroes in on Jesus' face, delirious with pain. (Jim Caviezel comments that he didn't have to do much acting at that point. "I was a mess. I was completely exhausted from the backbreaking schedule that the flagellation make-up made me follow that week. The weather was bitter cold, and there I was in a loincloth. And to top it all off there was a flu bug going around, and I had just picked it up. After we shot that scene I had the doctor take my temperature and it was over the top. They sent me home and I slept for three days straight.") Out of the corner of His swollen eye Jesus sees one of His torturers' sandals, sprinkled with His own blood. It reminds Him of other sandals—His Apostles'.

During the Last Supper, the Gospels record that the Apostles were talking amongst themselves about the positions they were going to occupy when Christ came into His Kingdom (they still hadn't understood the true nature of Christ's Kingdom). Overhearing the discussion, Jesus decided to use the occasion to teach them a lesson in Christian leadership. He got up from the table, wrapped a towel around His waist, and proceeded to wash His Apostles' feet.

In first century Palestine, washing someone else's feet was a chore reserved only for slaves. Among Jews at the time it was considered so degrading that the Sanhedrin had requested an exemption from this chore for Jewish slaves throughout the Empire. Their request had been granted.

Conditions in the ancient world compounded the natural humiliation involved in washing someone else's feet. Most of the roads were dirt, used by pack and riding animals as well as shepherds and dairy farmers bringing their flocks to market, so a variety of manures worked its way in with the dirt. Sandals protected the soles of your feet but were open on top; even a brief walk could coat your feet and ankles with the putrid mud lining the road. Foot-washing was necessary, and such a menial chore was reserved for slaves to do.

When Jesus washed His Apostles' feet at the Last Supper, they were understandably shocked, even ashamed. When He was finished, He explained the lesson behind His gesture:

> *Then after he had washed their feet and taken his garments, being set down again, he said to them: Know you what I have done to you? You call me Master and Lord. And you say well: for so I am. If then I being your Lord and Master, have washed your feet; you also ought to wash one another's feet. For I have given you an example, that as I have done to you, so you do also. Amen, amen, I say to you: The servant is not greater than his lord: neither is the apostle greater than he that sent him.*[67]

Jesus had given them a living parable of humility, of the importance of striving not to exalt oneself, but to serve one another. On the hard stone floor of the flagellation loggia, as Jesus gazed at His blood staining the guards' feet, the film brings the lesson out again. Christ's sacrifice of His dignity and His life during the Passion (symbolized by the spilling of His blood), is an act of service for all men and women of all times and places, even for those who are torturing Him at the time. His blood spattering on His enemy's sandals is the extension, the fulfillment even, of the washing of His Apostles' feet, His ultimate act of self-sacrificing service to the human

67 John 13:12-16.

race. His obedience to the Father, the shedding of His blood, will cleanse the human race of its disobedience to God, and bring them back into friendship with God.

The flashbacks are more than cinematic strokes of brilliance; they also are deep theological truths.

MAGDALENE'S FLASHBACK

The blood spilled at the flagellation sets off another flashback—Magdalene's. When Jesus' mother, Mary, kneels down and begins wiping up her son's blood, Magdalene spontaneously kneels down beside her. Without exchanging words, the women know that as impractical as it seems, it is the right thing to do. Jesus is their Lord, the one they revere and love, the one who is giving His life—His blood—for them. This gentle gesture is an antidote to their feeling of helplessness.

This too was an idea gleaned from Sister Emmerich's meditations.[68] Once again the film enhances it, having the two women perform the same action with very different attitudes. Mary, using the linens she received from Claudia Procles, begins to work with strong, motherly determination. Though there are plenty of linens, Magdalene removes her own veil and uses it as she kneels down to help. Her attitude is more one of reverence and devotion. In that context she remembers her first encounter with Jesus, the encounter that transformed her life.

Using her veil highlights that this is an intensely personal gesture for Magdalene; it is the moment when her hero has just been dragged away, and

---

68 The gesture is reminiscent of the care the Jewish priests took in wiping up the blood of the sacrifices in the Temple, and the care Christian priests take in purifying the chalice after the sacrifice of the Mass. Perhaps this is the reason it appeared in Sister Emmerich's meditations, whether or not it actually happened. It is reminiscent of the long-standing Catholic devotion to "The Most Precious Blood" of Jesus.

she remembers why He's her hero. It's as if His blood reminds her of how He defended her against those who wanted to shed her blood. She's engaged in the moment. She sees Jesus' mother cleaning up the blood. She can hardly believe that Mary even has the composure to do it. John really can't believe it; he simply starts to weep. He loses his composure; it's too much for him. Seeing Jesus' mother cleaning up the blood is more than he can bear. But Magdalene has the courage to get down by Mary's side and join her. She remembers her relationship to that blood, how it saved her. And she goes back in her mind to a literal rescue, where her life was saved—not only her spiritual life, but even her physical life.

In the flashback, the film identifies Magdalene with the famous "adulterous woman" from chapter eight of John's Gospel—something the Gospels themselves do not do. What the Gospels do record is that Magdalene is a devoted follower of Jesus; He cast seven demons out of her—more than that the Gospels don't record. The adulterous woman is not even named in the Gospel. She was supposedly caught in the act of adultery, and some of the Pharisees took advantage of the opportunity to trap Jesus. They brought her in front of Him, reminded Him that the Mosaic Law required that she be stoned to death, and left Him to make the decision.

This was one of many attempts of Jesus' enemies to discredit Him in the eyes of the populace: if He agreed to the stoning, it would cancel His reputation as merciful and forgiving; if He didn't, He could be labeled an unfaithful follower of God's law. Jesus, as usual, avoids the trap and uses the occasion to invite His critics to repentance. After bending down to draw in the dirt, He says to the crowd, "He that is without sin among you, let him first cast a stone at her," then He goes back to writing in the dirt. St. John describes how that comment took the wind out of the self-righteous mob: the older men walked away first, and after a bit of hesitation the younger men followed. When all of them have gone, Jesus turns to the woman and asks her if any of them had condemned her. She answers that they haven't, and Jesus says, "Neither will I condemn thee; go and now sin no more."

A CINEMATIC HOME RUN

It's one of the most arresting visual moments in the film. The flashback isn't specifically theological; it's a flash of dramatic beauty that echoes the moral beauty of the moment (forgiveness and salvation). At first, you don't know exactly what's going on, but the bright sequence of images draws you in: the close-up of the finger digging in the dirt and cutting right across the screen, in slow motion, and the angry mob in the background, out of focus, and the dust flying up—it's a gripping sequence.

Volumes have been written about the theological significance of every detail in the scene as it appears in St. John's Gospel, not the least the nature of His mysterious writing in the dirt (a venerable opinion surmises that Jesus was cataloguing the Pharisees' sins). But the fundamental message emerges loud and clear even without theological speculation: Jesus is the one who has no sin; He is the only one with the right to throw the first stone. But He doesn't, He gives the sinner a chance to repent. "For I am not come to call the just, but sinners.... I came not to judge the world, but to save the world," Jesus had explained.[69]

Most biblical scholars, and even the majority of Christian tradition, disagree with the film's fusing of these two figures in the Gospels, Magdalene and the adulterous woman. There's nothing to say for sure she was the woman who was going to be stoned, but then again there's nothing to say for certain that she wasn't. Literally speaking, it could have been her. The film

69 Matthew 9:13; John 12:47.

makes the connection, however, because in one way or another Jesus did save Magdalene, just as He saved the adulterous woman. The two had had the same experience: a saving encounter with Christ's forgiveness. And both had used it to change the direction of their lives. Jesus' love had given Magdalene new hope, and that hope fed her faith in Him, even as she saw with her own eyes and touched with her own hands the blood representing His apparent defeat.

THE CROWNING WITH THORNS

Originally the crowning with thorns was slated to be even more disfiguring by showing a thorn coming through Jesus' eyelid. But that detail didn't get past the editing process—it was determined that it was bad enough in its original form. To intensify the action even more would have incited a real stampede out of the screening room.

That editorial decision coincides with the Christian tradition's understanding of what this action means. More than a mere increase in physical torment, the crowning also signifies another type of suffering, another mode of rejecting Christ, and therefore another genre of sin: mockery, disrespect, humiliation. The crown of thorns added to Christ's physical suffering, but treating Him like a mock king added even more to His moral suffering. In truth He is the King, from a Christian standpoint, the generous King who offers inner peace and spiritual prosperity to those who embrace His merciful justice. The crown of thorns, the "royal" robe, the makeshift scepter—they create another devilish distortion of that awe-inspiring truth.

The mockery also calls to mind the anguish and sorrow that people cause one another through careless and uncharitable speech. The soldiers add insulting words and gestures to their burlesque. An insult spoken in jest, an envious word of derision whispered behind someone's back, gossip spread out of jealousy—these sins too Jesus took upon Himself. They wounded His sensitive heart as painfully as the thorns pierced the sensitive skin of His forehead.

THE VERDICT

As Pilate reluctantly gives in to the fury of the crowd, he symbolically expresses his misgivings by washing his hands. When Jesus sees the basin of water, He enters another flashback. You see Jesus preparing the bread and wine at the start of the Last Supper, and then washing His own hands as the ritual meal begins. During that meal, Jesus institutes the ritual sacrifice of the New Covenant, the sacrifice that will be celebrated by the Christian Church in "the breaking of the bread,"[70] as the New Testament later refers to it. It is a ceremony that still forms the heart of the Mass to this day.

Why does the film include this flashback? It wasn't in the script; the idea came while they were filming, as a way to help viewers contemplate the significance of Pilate's verdict in relation to the Passover ritual. When Pilate pronounces his verdict, it's the real beginning of Christ's execution, the official beginning of His death. His death was the sacrifice that fulfilled the Old Covenant (where the lamb was sacrificed before the Passover meal) and established the New Covenant (where Christ Himself was the sacrificial lamb). Furthermore, at His Last Supper (His last Passover supper), Jesus had already instituted the *ritual*, the way in which that sacrifice would be extended in time, through the Mass. So the two handwashings are really the same thing: the first action in the killing of the sacrificial victim. The sacrifice is starting; the lamb has been cut; it's bleeding; now it will be immolated.

70 Cf. Acts 2:42.

PART III: THE EXECUTION

CHAPTER 7

✦ ✠ ✦

ROAD TO CALVARY

Calvary is the name of the hilltop outside Jerusalem where Jesus was crucified. In Aramaic the place was called Golgotha, which means "skull" (the
shape of the hill resembled a head or a skull, and criminals were usually
executed there; also, an ancient Jewish tradition speculates that Adam had
been buried there). Criminals condemned to crucifixion had to carry their
own crosses (or at least the crossbar—scholarship and tradition purport various theories about the details) along a well known route through the streets
of Jerusalem. The route was about a mile long, passed through narrow alleys
(mostly uphill), out one of the city gates, and up to Calvary. This added
humiliation to the torture of their punishment, since jeering crowds would
line the way. The public display also helped deter would-be criminals, or so
the authorities hoped.

In the years following Christ's Passion and Resurrection, the early
Christian community commemorated the path that Jesus walked bearing His
cross by retracing His steps in an atmosphere of prayer and penance. Even in
the later years of the Roman Empire, Christian pilgrims to the Holy Land

recorded in their diaries and letters the profound emotion and piety they felt when they joined these processions. The practice of retracing Christ's steps, spiritually accompanying Him during His death march, has endured even to this day. In Catholic Churches today a series of paintings or relief sculptures depicting the most poignant moments of this sorrowful journey are a constant reminder. Both the journey and the pious devotion are known as "The Way of the Cross," (in Latin, *Via Crucis*) or the "Stations of the Cross."

The Gospels record some details about it: Jesus carried His own cross, at least part of the way; He was helped by a visitor to Jerusalem named Simon of Cyrene; two other criminals were also heading to Calvary for execution; and Jesus spoke to some women who accompanied Him, sorrowing and lamenting. Tradition records other aspects: He encountered His mother, Mary, along the way; a disciple named Seraphia (better known by her later name of St. Veronica) wiped His face as He passed by; He fell multiple times—exhausted from the physical torture, hounded by the soldiers, crushed by the weight of the cross. Other details surface here and there in devotional writings, but these have been preserved with the greatest historical certainty.

THE WEIGHT OF THE CROSS

Most contemporary scholars argue that the Romans constructed a wooden scaffolding on Calvary, and criminals condemned to crucifixion would be attached to a single crossbar hoisted onto the scaffolding. If this were the case, Christ should have carried only the crossbar, which would have been laid on His shoulders and held by ropes that forced His arms around it. The film accepted this scenario for the two thieves crucified with Jesus, but preferred to stick with the more familiar image of Jesus carrying His completely constructed cross. Two considerations went into that decision.

First, Anne Catherine Emmerich described a situation where they only had two patibula (scaffoldings) ready. Two were enough for the thieves, but for Jesus they had to scrounge around the night before and put together a whole cross, a one-piece contraption. That also explained, in her meditations, why Pilate was able to tack up a plaque detailing the crime on the top of Jesus' cross. Ordinarily they just hung a sign around the criminal's neck.

Sister Emmerich's version made the contrast in cross-carrying methods on the road to Calvary plausible, but another factor clinched the final decision. Symbolically and artistically, the film was compelled to show Jesus carrying the whole cross—that is the ubiquitous image portrayed throughout Christian art and iconography. That deeply engrained image is how people see it in their minds.

If true, Christ's cross is at least twice as heavy as the thieves' crosses. It's so heavy that even Simon of Cyrene, the passerby enlisted to help Jesus with His burden, can barely support the weight of the cross. Jesus, weakened from torture and great loss of blood, would not have had the physical strength to carry the solid wooden cross even for a few steps. Yet somehow, the viewer accepts it, due in part, to Jim Caviezel's remarkable performance. He combines total weakness with total determination. How was he able to be so convincing? "The cross we used was heavy, so that helped. But the real cross would have been almost three times as heavy.[71] I just had to think of that, and I did what He would have done."

The filmmakers took an educated guess at the actual size: 15 x 8 feet, close to 250 pounds, comparable to the weight of several railroad ties. Dragging it on the ground would have shifted some of the weight off Jesus' shoulders. Still, it would have been crushingly uncomfortable. You can't help but

71 The cross used in filming was only a prop; an actual cross of full weight would have impeded the choreography and multiple takes.

wonder whether Jesus would have been able to carry it after having suffered so much already. Perhaps some divine assistance was required. But since the experts themselves can't agree, the film had ample parameters within which to elaborate its own artistic rendering.

Perhaps the film wasn't purposely trying to put forth a theological statement with this choice, but it does so anyway. In Christian spirituality the devastating weight of the cross is often symbolically equated with the weight of mankind's sins, the sins which Christ took upon Himself for the salvation of the human family. As God, Christians believe, Jesus was able to take the sins of every person onto Himself and obliterate them through the sacrifice of His crucifixion. But as man, it was painful—that's what the Passion is all about. That Jesus' cross weighed twice as much as the thieves' crosses, from this perspective, graphically expresses a theological nuance: the thieves had to carry only the burden of their own sins; Christ carried the much heavier burden of everyone's sins.

CHRIST'S CROSS AND OURS

Crucifixion was a common form of execution in Jesus' day. Everyone was familiar with the frightening image of condemned criminals stumbling through the streets under the crushing weight of their instrument of execution, following one after another like a hellish chain gang. Some modern scholars even explain that when multiple criminals were being marched off to crucifixion, they were actually tied together in single file by a rope, to make it easier to keep them moving along in an orderly fashion.

Before His own crucifixion, Jesus mentioned this horribly vivid image when He was preaching, not merely to spice up a sermon or two, but to describe the very essence of Christian living. The Gospels of Matthew, Mark, and Luke all record Jesus summing up what it means to be His disciple in the same way: "And he said to all, 'If any man would come after me, let him deny himself and take up his cross daily and follow me.'" Being a Christian involves carrying one's own cross every day, just as Christ carried His cross to Calvary. Are all Christians therefore supposed to seek literal execution by crucifixion? Not exactly; Jesus elaborates on His own analogy: "For whoever would save his life will lose it; and whoever loses his life for my sake, he will save it. For what does it profit a man if he gains the whole world and loses or forfeits himself?"[72]

In this teaching, Jesus interprets beforehand the significance of the Way of the Cross. In God's plan of salvation it was necessary for Jesus to deny His own natural will for survival and embrace death by crucifixion. It was a difficult path to take, but Jesus' love and trust in the Father led Him down it. As He stumbles and weaves through Jerusalem hearing the insults of the crowd, and enduring the whipping of the guards and the weight of His cross, He is teaching His disciples a powerful lesson. Following God's will (living according to faith, hope, love, and forgiveness) in a world ruled by selfishness and greed will not always be easy. But followers of Jesus must stay strong and forge ahead, trusting in the power of love, just as He does, no matter how heavy the cross becomes. The Way of the Cross is a living parable for Christian discipleship, a parable that can give meaning to every struggle and sorrow on the path of life.

The film highlights this at the start of the sequence. Christ's cross is dropped to the ground in front of Him with a thud, hushing the noise of the crowd. Seeing the cross, Jesus steps toward it, falls to His knees, and embraces it—pressing His bloodstained cheek tenderly against it, like a lover's embrace. He prays, "O Lord, I am thy servant, the son of thy handmaid."

---

72 Luke 9:23-25; cf. Matthew 16:24-26 and Mark 8:34-37.

Another quotation from the Psalms,[73] it calls to mind the prayer in Gethsemane and the prayer before His scourging—it is the New Adam, continuing His loving obedience, His rehabilitation of the human family's broken trust in God.

THE PASSION'S OK CORRAL

As the sequence begins and the condemned criminals make their way through the gate and into the street, Satan makes his second-to-last appearance in the film. It's another one of those powerful, wordless scenes, a judicious on-site addition to the screenplay. You see the Devil on one side of the gauntlet and Mary on the other, outside the gate. Both of them are moving with the procession of criminals. And then, right in the middle of all the bustle and activity, they see each other. They really look at each other. It was something the filmmakers planned only a day or two before they shot it.

Why include it? Because it turns the tables: the Mother faces off with the Devil, and it's frightening—for the Devil. Mary represents the realm of fidelity and faith, and Satan recognizes it. That's the important thing about that scene: that strange figure in the crowd (the Devil) recognizes who and what Mary is. In the face-off, Mary gets the better of the Devil—she looks away first. Satan begins to realize, for the first time, that he may not be winning.

It can be seen as the moment when Satan fears the fulfillment of the prophecy recorded in the Book of Genesis—the same prophecy that inspired the snake-crushing scene in Gethsemane: "I will put enmities between thee [the Devil] and the woman, and thy seed and her seed; she shall crush thy head, and thou shalt lie in wait for her heel." In the original Hebrew there is some ambiguity about whose heel, that of the woman or that of her progeny

73 Psalm 115:16.

(her "seed"). Translations differ on this point. But some of the longest standing translations, and much of popular Catholic piety, refer to the woman's heel.

Jesus never looks at the Devil. The only person in the entire film who sees that evil presence is Mary. It is both fascinating and full of impact. Satan is cocky in his invisibility, but then Mary sees him, stares him down, and dismisses him. It's as if she says, *Yes, I know you're there, but there's something more important going on right now. I'll deal with you later.*

Christian spirituality considers the forces of good and evil unequally matched; good is infinitely stronger, even though evil often seems to have its way. The visual combat between Mary and Satan gets that message across, right when evil ought to be rejoicing—another sign of hope.

WHEN CHRIST FALLS
Jesus falls and gets up six times during the film's Way of the Cross. The movie strives to make each fall unique. At the same time, each fall has two things in common with all the others: they exhibit the total depletion of Christ's physical strength, and they manifest the extent of His love. Nothing can keep Him from drinking the cup His Father has given Him, nothing. For Jesus, the salvation of sinners matters more than anything, even more than the limits His human nature would put on the degree of His self-sacrifice. Jesus could have called those "twelve legions of angels" to His aid; He could have rebelled against His Father's seemingly unreasonable plan. But His love endured, His hope in the Father's goodness stayed steady—steadier than His own legs, which collapsed beneath Him over and over again.

Through the centuries, this heroic demonstration of love has been a continual source of strength for Christians. Christ's physical falls are often correlated to the spiritual falls of His disciples—their sins, their failings, their moral weaknesses. In Christ's unrelenting determination to reach Calvary, His followers renew their hope. They are confident that if Christ suffered so much to redeem them, He will gladly forgive them if they ask to be forgiven. Christians can always find in Christ's falls a motivation to pick themselves up and begin their lives of discipleship again, and again, and again.

The film heightens this meaning of Christ's falls by demonstrating the effect they have on certain individuals around Him; these moments of His dire weakness produce strength in others.

A MOTHER'S CHALLENGE

Mary is the first one to go through this process. The crowd closes in behind Jesus as He moves forward, and Mary is pushed back; she can't see Him. She turns to John, "Get me close to Him." John knows the streets well, leading Mary and Magdalene out of the crowd, down a side street, and back up to the main route where Jesus will pass. Ahead of the crowd, they reach the intersection the moment the thieves appear. Mary is winded by the dash, and she pauses in a doorway. Her face reflects that more than physical fatigue is holding her back. It seems as if she doesn't have the courage to do what she came there for, to comfort her son. Jesus suddenly appears, dragging Himself forward, but Mary remains paralyzed. She still cannot muster the strength to go to Him. Then He loses his footing and collapses under the huge cross. His fall jumpstarts her love. With motherly devotion she throws herself toward her son, embracing Him and adding what strength she has left to His.

The film punctuates this heartrending struggle with another flashback. A younger Mary runs to comfort her little boy—Jesus—after an accidental fall. Juxtaposing the pristine innocence and serene delicacy of the flashback with the brutal, bloody chaos of the Via Dolorosa makes this perhaps the most moving of all the flashbacks. It adds emotional dimension to the crucial real-time scene between Mary and Jesus.

While Mary, Magdalene, and John were running through the back streets to get ahead of the procession, Mary momentarily had lost sight of Jesus. She unwittingly allowed herself to be let down emotionally; in a sense, it put some distance between herself and the horror. When the three see Jesus, the thought of having to go and grapple with the gruesome reality again was more than Mary could take. But then Jesus falls. Mary's reluctance snaps as she realizes that her son is in trouble. It's as if she says to herself, *He's in trouble. I have to go to him; I'm His mother and I can't let anything stand in the way of helping Him, comforting Him. I've got to at least try to go to Him just to show Him that I'm there.*

After the filming they dubbed in a line, which Maia never actually said on camera, to express those same feelings. Mary presses through the crowd and puts her arms around Jesus and says, "I'm here." She repeats it again: "I'm here. " The first time the words are desperate, the second time, sweet. All she needs to do is simply be there for Him. That's a mother's love; that's Mary's faith. The flashback emphasizes this inner struggle and resolution. Still she needed to be reminded of her duty, of her role. She was the mother of God, but she was also a real human being. It took all her mother's love to endure it.

Jesus rewards her gesture of love, strengthening her even as she strengthens Him, by reminding her of the meaning behind His hideous torture. Rising to His feet, He looks her in the eye and says, "Behold, Mother, I make all things new!" This quote is taken from the last book of the New

Testament, the Apocalypse.[74] It refers to the final victory of Christ over evil, the end of history when, Christians believe, He will come again to judge the living and the dead.

The verse in the Apocalypse preceding the line Jesus speaks in the film explains symbolically the difference between the "new creation" that will be fulfilled at that time and the fallen creation that precedes it: "… And God shall wipe away all tears from their eyes, and death shall be no more. Nor mourning, nor crying, nor sorrow shall be any more, for the former things are passed away." By including that line ("Behold, I make all things new"), the film shows Jesus reminding Mary, who is entirely (and understandably) absorbed by her son's terrible sufferings, that the suffering isn't the end of the story. Rather, it is the path to freedom and eternal joy for her and for all sinners.

Co-screenwriter Benedict Fitzgerald believed that even though the line was not part of the Gospel's account, it seemed to fit well. When Icon Productions screened the first version to an auditorium of four hundred Jesuit priests in Los Angeles, that line threw them into a chorus of affirmation. They loved it; they saw it as the climax of the film, the perfect touch. When the Savior of the world needs His mother's help to get back on His feet and continue His redeeming journey, a powerful line of Scripture added to a script flashes like a bolt of lightning to reveal the meaning of human history.

VERONICA'S ANGELIC COURAGE

Christ's fall stirred up Mary's love and increased her faith and hope. A later fall does the same for Seraphia (St. Veronica). The name Seraphia hearkens back to the name the Bible gives to one of the orders of angels, the sera-

---

74 Apocalypse 21:5.

phim.[75] The film indeed makes her appear angelic. In a sense, it's one of the most spiritual moments of the film. The oldest Christian traditions chronicling the Way of the Cross record this encounter, though the Gospel writers don't mention it. Seraphia wiped Jesus' face with her veil, a courageous act of kindness and compassion in the midst of His hideous journey. Christ rewarded her by leaving His image on the veil through the stains of His blood and sweat.[76]

The veil symbolizes Christ's intimate, personal love for His disciples, and His approval of every self-sacrificing act of kindness and service. St. Veronica has inspired generations of Christians to imitate her charity by serving their suffering neighbors. In the context of the Passion, however, the film insinuates other levels of meaning as well.

The music, the film speed, and the lighting combine to present a dreamlike sequence, a tactic used to express an invisible, spiritual reality (the heart-to-heart substance of this encounter) in a visible way. Veronica strolls right through a chaotic melee, filled with a serene joy and exuding an inner beauty, completely focused on Jesus and oblivious to the risk she's taking. It was as if Christ was drawing her towards Him, invisibly opening up a path for her. The filmmakers had a tough time making it work. The extras were trying to do a noisy, confusing shot, and she was trying to achieve an ethereal ballet-like moment, floating along like an angel. The extras kept bumping

75 See Isaiah, chapter 6.

76 According to historical records, Christians have venerated the cloth since at least the time of Constantine (early fourth century); earlier records are few and far between, due to the repeated waves of Roman persecution that destroyed Christian documents. The veil was kept in St. Peter's Basilica in Rome until 1600, when it disappeared under odd circumstances. Currently, many Christians believe it to be kept in a village in central Italy called Manopello, where they continue to venerate it as a physical link to Christ's Passion. Seraphia's more familiar name of Veronica stems from the image He left on her veil: *Vera icona* is Latin for true image.

into her, over and over again. In multiple takes the crowd was directed not to touch her, let alone bump into her. Consequently the extras fell into awkward movements, swirling right up to Seraphia and then stopping. That didn't work either.

In the end, it came out exactly as the script envisioned it. Seraphia is oblivious to everything going on around her and walks with focus and purpose, as if being summoned. In a sense, it's a strange sequence, but for that very reason it works. *What's she doing?* you think the first time you see her. You don't know why she's even in the movie. She appears with no explanation, radiating a simple, inner beauty. She's calmly preparing some wine. *Who is she?* She diverts the attention from the gruesome drama. The sequence becomes a mini-mystery, a suspenseful subplot.

But Seraphia does more than add dramatic and aesthetic layers to the film; she represents all of Christ's disciples who were too scared to support Him publicly that day. Everyone, all the disciples, anyone who was a friend of Jesus, was hiding, except Mary and Magdalene and John. Most of them were taking Peter's out: *Hey, we don't even know that man.* Anne Catherine Emmerich explains that they didn't want to end up getting hounded, hunted, and condemned themselves. They're all lying low. The remarkable thing about Seraphia, therefore, is that she defied everyone—the soldiers, the crowd—to walk up and comfort that man when He fell.

Perhaps this is why Christian tradition has held so adamantly to the memory of this encounter, even though it doesn't appear in the Bible. Seraphia overcame the fears inhibiting Christ's other disciples. That alone suggests a supernatural boost to her courage. She could have been manhandled by the soldiers, but she pays them no mind. Her utter fearlessness foreshadows the coming of the Holy Spirit at Pentecost, when He activates that same attitude in the Apostles.

The look Jim Caviezel gives her when she kneels in front of him to offer the drink captures the spiritual connection perfectly. Somehow, in the midst of Jesus' unbearable pain, those eyes tell you that He is thinking more of her, of her courage and her love, of her generosity, than of Himself. In His eyes is an immense wave of silent gratitude. His love and her faith meet, producing an icon of hope: His image on her veil. It is a perfect instance of what co-screenwriter Benedict Fitzgerald called the secret of the film's genius, its "marriage of majesty and intimacy."

Some of the earliest Christian sermons still in existence elaborate on the idea that in Christ's Passion God made Himself weak on purpose, so that He would have to depend on others, calling forth in them the courage of love and faith, just as He did for Veronica. The Christian Church has long taught that God continues this, permitting (though not willing) suffering and injustice, so that everyone can have a chance to be like Veronica by serving Christ in weak and suffering brethren. Christ continues to imprint His portrait, not on a veil, but on compassionate hearts.

CONSPICUOUSLY ABSENT: THE PIOUS WOMEN OF JERUSALEM AND THE DEVIL

When Icon Productions screened early versions of the film to groups of Christian ministers and clergy, some of them questioned why the film includes the extra-biblical encounter with Veronica, but excludes Christ's biblical encounter with the pious women of Jerusalem, who were walking beside Him along the way and lamenting His suffering.[77] In the Gospels Jesus says, "Weep not over me; but weep for yourselves and for your children." In

---

77 See Luke 23:27-31.

the film the women are there all along the way, crying and sobbing. And the brief conversation was filmed. But in the end, it seemed more of an interruption to the drama rather than an asset. The sequence was already long because of all the falls; it couldn't afford to be stopped in its tracks with that small exchange.

And the Devil? After the showdown with Mary, the Devil lies low until the final defeat at the end. Considering the extreme violence of the soldiers throughout the Way of the Cross sequence, it would have been understandable to include a shot or two of Satan, mingling gleefully with the scornful torturers. Once again, artistic reasons took precedence. Less is more. If the Devil is overused, it gets distracting. Intuitively, you know that the Devil is there the whole time. You don't need to keep seeing him.

SIMON OF CYRENE'S RELUCTANT REDEMPTION

No one follows Christ so closely throughout the sequence as Simon of Cyrene, the innocent bystander recruited to help Jesus carry His cross. And no one is so reluctant to do so. He wants nothing to do with a condemned man on the eve of a religious holiday (the Sabbath was beginning that evening, and the Jewish Passover, the most sacred annual holiday, had already begun). It takes the threats of the Roman in charge and the pitiful pleas of some sorrowful women ("Help him! He's a holy man!") to convince Simon to take his place beside the repulsive figure of Jesus. Simon's face reflects a mixture of horror, disgust, and fear as he shoulders the cross together with Jesus. The recruit from the crowd bears most of the cross's weight himself, while Christ's arm locks with his around the beam.

Simon is one of the film's most compelling characters. He represents all of us. He doesn't want to step out of his comfort zone and into a costly relationship with Jesus. He sees it going on and he doesn't want to be there.

He recognizes the danger in it, and the humiliation of it; he's worried about what people will think. He just doesn't want to do it; he wants them to leave him alone. But in the end, he's actually more afraid not to do it.

It's a portrait of Everyman. Everyone is called to follow the path of integrity and authentic love, but no one wants want to do it. The cost seems too high; it's too painful. Often people need to be coerced by circumstances into actually doing what they're supposed to do, which, somehow, is a gift from God. Sometimes you need to get burned in order to be turned in the right direction. What New Age calls "karmic retribution" can also be called a solid reminder from God. As the reminders add up, the will is gradually turned around to where it should be. It takes a certain amount of resignation, but the result is freedom gained.

This is a no-frills vision of the spiritual and moral life, played out convincingly in Simon of Cyrene. It's an experience of reluctant redemption, and it explains why Simon gets so much camera time. At first it's sheer willpower, he has to force himself to do what he needs to do. But something happens to him along the way. Simon changes. Actually, it's Jesus; Jesus changes him. They don't have a long philosophical talk about the meaning of life, but they do communicate.

Jesus gives Simon a look, right from His heart, not just once, but multiple times. And Simon gets it. He gets what Jesus is about—love, self-sacrifice. It's as if Jesus lights up something inside of Simon. At the end Simon can't tear himself away. The guards tell him to get out, but he stays there, staring at Jesus. Carrying the cross with Christ changed him. It taught him about real love, love that gives till it hurts. That experience made a believer out of him; Christ's love gave him faith. It was Simon's experience; it can be anyone's.

The scene depicting Jesus and Simon arriving at Calvary is co-screenwriter Benedict Fitzgerald's favorite moment in the entire film. Jesus collapses to the ground, and Simon throws the cross off to the side, collapsing himself as he keeps the cross from crushing Jesus. His face is close to Christ's and they look at each other. The Roman guard tells Simon he can go, but he can't tear his eyes away from Jesus. He doesn't want to leave. He just stays there and stares at Jesus. As Benedict Fitzgerald explains: "In that moment there is such a communion between those two men. Such intimacy. That moment has stayed with me. I think about it often, almost with envy. To me, that is the secret to the film's power: somehow it combines majesty and intimacy."

When the Gospel of Mark mentions Simon of Cyrene, it also mentions the names of his children, Alexander and Rufus. Christians have long believed (and secondary sources seem to confirm it), that these two men eventually became pillars of the early Christian community. Tradition extrapolates that Simon himself must have become a follower of Christ after his encounter on the road to Calvary. Witnessing that encounter from the film's perspective, with the silent, intimate exchanges Simon has with Jesus as they stumble forward together, clumsily, painfully, inelegantly, one sees clearly why. Simon is the perfect antithesis to Pilate and Herod. He too was forced to look into the mysterious Savior's eyes, but he listened to what his heart told him about that look. As a result, hope was born.

TWO SERMONS ON THE MOUNT

As Jesus passes out through the city walls He glimpses Calvary, where soldiers are preparing for the crucifixions. Eyeing that accursed hilltop makes Him think of another hill immortalized by the Gospels, the hill back home in Galilee where He delivered, according to St. Matthew, the Sermon on the Mount. Once again, the film cuts to another crucial flashback.

Scholars generally agree that the Sermon on the Mount as it appears in chapters five through seven of St. Matthew's Gospel comprises a compendium of Christ's teaching. It is uncertain whether He delivered that actual sermon at that actual time. It is certain that the sermon contains the main points of all His preaching and teaching throughout the three years of public ministry before His Passion. It can be considered the "Cliff Notes" of Christ's doctrine.

Above all the Sermon on the Mount emphasizes humble trust in God and unconditional love for one's neighbor—for all one's neighbors, whether enemies or friends. The lines Jesus speaks in the brief flashback bring out those precise points:

> *But I say to you, love your enemies, do good to them that hate you, and pray for them that persecute and calumniate you, that you may be the children of your Father who is in heaven [who maketh his sun to rise upon the good, and bad, and raineth upon the just and the unjust]. For if you love those who love you, what reward shall you have?*[78]

It was important to emphasize this, to see as clearly as possible the meaning behind Christ's suffering. It's not just a "grin and bear it" type of pain. The real message of the Passion comes from the example that Christ gives, the flawless translation into His own actions of what He had meant with His words. The visual contrast offered by the flashback—a frayed, bloody, barely recognizable human being versus a strong, vibrant, commanding leader—not only emphasizes the lesson, it seems to teach it in a whole new way. It's not mere words about loving one's enemies; Jesus embodies the message with vigor and meaning.

78 Matthew 5:44-46.

Artistic and spiritual intuitiveness inspired not only the choice of lines, but also the way Jim Caviezel expresses them. The original screenplay didn't include this flashback. It was added during post-production. The wide-angle shot was filmed outside Rome, but the final close-up was done in a soundstage in Los Angeles. During the soundstage session, Jim delivered the same line almost one hundred times. He eventually nailed the right expressive combination. It definitely needed to have a sense of seriousness, because the message is serious—you can't get much heavier. But at the same time it had to have a dash of something else.

What was this other ingredient? While they were filming, Jim experimented with different deliveries. They didn't stumble on the right feeling until Jim was reminded that he was delivering the "Good News." Suddenly, Jim threw in more enthusiasm, a tinge of joy, while still maintaining the message's gravity. The flashback does provide a flash of joy, of warmth before returning back to the final steps of the Way of the Cross up Mount Calvary. But Calvary looks different after the brief journey to the Sermon on the Mount; the joy of the flashback lingers and sweetens the sorrow of the suffering. Once again, hope emerges.

CAIAPHAS IS LET OFF THE HOOK

Jesus reaches Calvary at the same time as Caiaphas and his retinue. The latter have come riding on donkeys (the traditional way for respected rabbis to travel in ancient Palestine), and so they have had to follow a different, longer route. As Jesus tops the hill, half-carried along by Simon of Cyrene together with the cross, He looks up towards the sun and sees the cold, hardened faces of Caiaphas and Annas staring down at Him. Their looks are mixed with approval at His punishment and disdain for Him. From their perspective, blasphemers deserve nothing less than what Jesus is getting. Christ recognizes them, but His look shows no resentment, no hatred. He doesn't blame them. The flashback inserted precisely at that point explains why.

"No man taketh it [His life] away from me," you hear Jesus explain. "But I lay it down of myself. And I have power to lay it down, and I have power to take it up again. This commandment have I received of my Father."[79] The film again emphasizes the reason behind Christ's sufferings: it's all part of the Father's plan. It's all in the plan for salvation. It's not as if Caiaphas and those other leaders had control over Jesus. They were doing their own thing, true, but there were other forces at work. That needed to be emphasized again, before they started crucifying Him. This flashback was a post-production addition too. They shot it in a parking lot, with Jim standing in the back of a pick-up truck, so the cameras could get the right angle on the flare of the afternoon sun.

ROOTS AND FRUITS OF CONTROVERSY:
FEARS OF ANTI-SEMITISM

As mentioned earlier, the Christian Church has always considered this voluntary nature of Christ's self-sacrifice an essential ingredient of man's redemption from sin: Adam's free act of self-indulgence led to the fall of the human race; Jesus' free act of self-giving redeems it. The film emphasizes this in various ways for the sake of truth in storytelling, but also for the sake of people who were concerned about the issue of blame.

When they were filming in Italy, some individuals and groups began publicly raising concern over the choice to do this film at all. Recalling past instances of Christian persecution against Jews, they wondered out loud whether a fresh, graphic depiction of Christ's execution might incite fresh outbursts of anti-Semitism under the auspices of berating all Jews as "Christ-

79 John 10:18.

against those who feared that the film would have a negative social impact.[83] The absence of violence in the wake of the film's release seems to have proven him right. In fact, *The Passion of The Christ* makes viewers recoil from the senselessness of all violence and injustice, just the opposite of inciting hatred and vengeance. As Cardinal Castrillon-Hoyos, prefect of the Vatican's Congregation for the Clergy, put it in an interview after a screening in Rome:

> Anti-Semitism, like all forms of racism, distorts the truth in order to put a whole race of people in a bad light. This film does nothing of the sort. It draws out from the historical objectivity of the Gospel narratives sentiments of forgiveness, mercy and reconciliation. It captures the subtleties and the horror of sin, as well as the gentle power of love and forgiveness, without making or insinuating blanket condemnations against one group. This film expresses the exact opposite, that learning from the example of Christ, there should never be any more violence against any other human being.[84]

With brilliant artistic and theological moments, such as Jesus flashing back to His public declaration that He will undergo His suffering and death voluntarily to carry out the Father's plan of salvation, the film reveals not only a personal vision of the Passion, but its truth. A truth inextricably intertwined with faith, hope, love, and forgiveness.

---

83 The very idea that a two-hour movie could generate a new outburst of anti-Semitic violence makes no sense. Those who feel hostile toward Jews and Judaism already know about the unflattering elements of the Gospels. ...Moreover, if you feel such hatred in your heart that a well-intentioned motion picture in Aramaic could inspire you to commit brutal attacks, then minor changes in that movie—trimming a line here, reediting a scene there—won't prevent that reaction. Quoted from "Mel's Masterpiece, Michael Medved, *London Evening Standard* (August 28, 2003).

84 Zenit News Agency, www.zenit.org ZE03091809.

CHAPTER 8

✠

THE CRUCIFIXION

HOW DID IT WORK?

Execution by crucifixion was invented by the ancient Phoenicians, a seafaring people who dominated Mediterranean commerce in the pre-Christian (and pre-Roman) era. For years they had experimented with different methods of capital punishment. Strangling, drowning, and immersion in boiling oil were effective deterrents to crime—at least for a time. And then the Phoenicians implemented the most effective method of all: crucifixion. It caused intense pain—nails were pounded through nerve bundles that led to the fingers and toes, so the excruciating pain of the initial piercing returned whenever the victim moved his hands or feet. It was impossible not to move—a person on a cross had to frequently push and pull himself up to breathe. Crucifixion was a slow death. In the end, either the condemned would die from thirst after two or three days (loss of blood would sometimes dehydrate them more quickly than usual, especially if they had been flogged prior to the crucifixion) or from suffocation, which could take up to four or five days. (Suffocation occurred when the victim no longer had enough physical strength or willpower to hoist himself up and expand his lungs to take a breath.)

During the long process of dying, the criminals were on public display. Everyone witnessed their repulsive fate—people and animals alike. Scavenging birds might devour the victims' flesh while they were still alive—there was no defense against the attacks. Insects tormented them; maggots would incubate and multiply in their open, festering wounds. The spectacle was so atrocious, so grotesquely degrading that Roman law forbade any full-fledged Roman citizen from being crucified; the punishment was reserved solely for condemned slaves and provincials. (This is why St. Peter was martyred by crucifixion in Rome around A.D. 64, but St. Paul, a Roman citizen, was executed in the same city at the same time by beheading.) When Christianity was finally legalized at the end of three centuries of Roman persecution, the emperor Constantine banned any artistic representations of Christ being crucified; the horrors of real crucifixions were simply too fresh in people's minds at the time.

Those working on the film did their homework on how crucifixion worked, but they found much the same thing they had found with the research on flagellation techniques: experts disagreed on the details. A series of judicious choices were in order.

Some of the early screenings sparked objections from those who believe that the Holy Shroud of Turin—considered by many to be the actual shroud in which Jesus was wrapped for burial—definitively shows the nail marks going through the wrists, not the palms of Jesus. The consultants for *The Passion of The Christ* granted a high level of validity to the Shroud, but they weren't so certain about the location of the nails. In fact, it's hard to tell because the Shroud only shows the back of the figure's hands.

Though some might bicker about the details of historicity, and even renowned experts will still fail to agree, one simple truth remains clear:

crucifixion was an atrociously painful and humiliating way to die. In the end, the film's choices about how to depict it were guided by research and a determination to be as faithful to history as possible.

SACRIFICE AND DESTRUCTION

Almost all brands of religion, from the most primitive to the most sophisticated, give center stage to the act of sacrifice. The word comes from the Latin *sacrum facere,* "to make holy." The concept connotes setting something valuable aside and offering it exclusively to God as an acknowledgment that God is all-powerful and all-good; the human community recognizes its need for divine help and protection. A praying community offering a sacrifice is saying to God, *You are the source of all life and goodness; we thank You and we ask You to continue sending us Your blessings.* By adding the sacrifice, the actual offering of some thing, mere words become material reality. For human beings, who exist in the material world, it makes perfect sense.

Through the act of sacrifice, mankind acknowledges dependence on God (for one's own existence, for fulfillment of that existence, and ultimately for the order of the universe outside of human control). But there is another side to religious sacrifice: the idea of destruction, of committing a violent act. Destroying something valuable leads to the step of making amends, of reparation. If you're sorry for wrecking your buddy's car, you will ask him to forgive you, but you will also feel obligated to help pay for the repairs. This innate sense of justice is fundamental to religion (and religion, in some form or another, has always been present in human society). It may only be superficial—trying to appease irrationally angry gods, for example—but it is always present.

This destructive aspect of religious sacrifice became the duty of the priest. The priest is the bridge between God and a particular human community. Priests perform the sacrifices in the name of the people. They enact the destruction of a valuable offering (the victim) as a sign of the people's gratitude, adoration, and penitence. The place where priest, victim, and people meet is the altar, the sacrificial stage.

In the Old Covenant, God Himself provided instructions for how His Chosen People, Israel, should offer sacrifices. He set aside an entire tribe to be Israel's priests, who administered different types of sacrificial activities, depending on the particular needs and desires of the faithful.[85] Prior to God's establishment of the priestly order, however, He chose individuals to be the caretakers of His blessing and His promise of salvation. These Patriarchs also performed sacrifices to honor Him.

For Christians, the Old Covenant sacrifices prefigured the one true sacrifice that was to come: Christ's self-sacrifice on the altar of the cross. The New Testament actually refers to the old sacrifices as "shadows of things to come."[86] They derived their value not from any intrinsic worth (what could God possibly get out of the sacrifice of a goat or bale of barley?), but from the faith and hope that accompanied them. They believed that God in His goodness and wisdom would somehow save sinful mankind from the broken world in which they found themselves.

FROM ABRAHAM AND ISAAC TO FATHER AND SON

One of the most eloquent Old Covenant images of Christ's future sacrifice appears in the story of Abraham, father of the People of Israel. God promised to make Abraham the father of a great nation and a blessing to all the peoples of the world. But there was a catch. God required Abraham to leave his homeland behind and essentially become a semi-nomad in order to

---

85 The book of Leviticus delineates these arrangements.
86 See Colossians 2:17.

receive the fulfillment of the promise. Abraham trusted God and set out for the land of Canaan, to Palestine. This was a tremendous act of faith. Accompanying Abraham was his wife, Sarah, who was barren; they were both advanced in age. Abraham and Sarah had no children, and humanly speaking the possibility seemed remote.

Abraham's journey led him through a series of remarkable and harrowing adventures. When he was a hundred years old and Sarah was ninety, they had their only son, Isaac, the child of the promise. (Isaac would eventually become the father of Jacob, and Jacob's twelve sons would become the fathers of the Twelve Tribes of Israel.) While Isaac was still a boy, God decided to put Abraham to the ultimate test. He asked him to go to Mount Moriah and offer his son, Isaac, as a burnt sacrifice to the Lord. No victim could be more precious to Abraham; no sacrifice would manifest his trust in God more fully. (Human sacrifice was still widespread among the peoples living in Palestine at this time, between 2000 and 1800 B.C.)

Abraham took Isaac up to Mount Moriah (which the Bible identifies as the location of what would later become the Temple Mount in Jerusalem[87]). He made Isaac carry the wood for the burnt sacrifice. When Isaac asked his father where the lamb for the sacrifice was, Abraham answered, "God himself will provide the lamb for the burnt offering, my son." Reaching the top of the hill, Abraham bound Isaac and laid him on the wood, unsheathed his knife, and laid it on his son's throat. The biblical text describes the heartrending moment briefly but vividly, with details that parallel the laying of Christ on the wood of the cross (wood which Christ, also the only son of His Father, had carried up the hill Himself), and the "binding" of His hands and feet by the nails:

87 And Solomon began to build the house of the Lord in Jerusalem, in mount Moria, which had been shewn to David his father, in the place which David had prepared in the thrashing floor of Ornan the Jebusite (2 Chronicles 3:1).

"And when they came to the place of which God had told him, Abraham built an altar there, and laid the wood in order, and bound Isaac his son, and laid him on the altar, upon the wood. Then Abraham put forth his hand, and took the knife to slay his son." The difference comes at that point. Whereas God the Father actually allowed the death of His Son, Jesus, He sent an angel to prevent Abraham from slaying Isaac, providing a ram instead.[88]

Christ's self-sacrifice was no mere ritual: He Himself was the only victim valuable enough to be a worthy offering to God, because He was both human and divine. God didn't care much about goats and barley, but He did care about His own Son. Christ was also the perfect victim because He had never sinned, He had never rebelled against God. He didn't deserve any punishment, yet He willingly offered Himself in place of all the children of Adam who had sinned. Finally, His self-offering out of love for the Father was the perfect prayer of adoration. In it He trusted His Father literally unto death.

THE LAST SUPPER FLASHBACKS

The early Christian community was comprised primarily of former Jews. The correlation between Christ's Passion and the Old Covenant rituals, types (or "images"), and prophecies convinced many Jews that Christ was the promised Messiah. The film connects the fulfillment of the Old Covenant prefigurations to the New Covenant sacrifice with the flashbacks that occur during the crucifixion sequence.

The Last Supper was Jesus' and His disciples' last Passover Seder. This ritual meal, celebrated each spring by the Jews, commemorated their

88 See Genesis, chapter 22.

liberation from slavery in Egypt and anticipated the advent of the promised Messiah.[89] Among the rich and beautiful symbolism of the ritual, three elements stand out: the lamb (sacrificed before the Seder and then eaten during the supper) and its blood, which was sprinkled on the doorposts so that the angel of death would pass over them; the unleavened bread, baked in haste (without leaven) before the Israelites' flight through the Red Sea; and four cups of wine, symbolizing the past, present, and future blessings poured forth by God on His Chosen People.

According to the New Testament and the practices of the early Christian Church, during the Last Supper Jesus altered the significance of these elements, making them refer to Himself and His self-sacrifice. He declared that the bread was no longer bread, but His flesh; the wine was no longer wine, but His blood. As St. Luke records it:

> *And taking bread, he gave thanks and brake and gave to them, saying, "This is my body, which is given for you. Do this for a commemoration of me. In like manner, the chalice also, after he had supped, saying: This is the chalice, the new testament in my blood, which shall be shed for you.*[90]

Obeying Christ's command to commemorate the Last Supper (known in New Testament terms as "the breaking of the bread"[91]) was from the start the central act of Christian worship. Jesus commanded His Apostles to perpetuate the new ritual; Christians continue the practice today.

---

89 Religious sacrifices often included a ritual meal—not only in ancient Israel—as a way for the people offering the sacrifice to participate in it more fully and also to express the reconciliation and communion the sacrifice effected between God and the sacrificing community.

90 Luke 22:19-20.

91 See Luke 24:35 and the Acts of the Apostles 2:42.

Catholic Christians have always understood Christ's command at the Last Supper in a sacramental way. In other words, during the Last Supper, Christ not only altered the symbolic meaning of the elements of the Passover Seder, but He actually altered their substance. The bread and wine not only came to symbolize His body and blood, which was about to be offered in sacrifice, but actually, mysteriously (*sacrament* comes from the Latin word for "mystery") became His body and blood, while maintaining the appearance of bread and wine. The Last Supper, therefore, was a real anticipation of Christ's saving self-sacrifice, which would take place the next day on Calvary.

Consequently, when the Apostles were commanded to commemorate the Last Supper, Catholics believe, they were also given the power to consecrate bread and wine into Christ's body and blood, and to ordain others with the same power. (This consecration is still today the heart of the Catholic Mass.) In this way, Christians of all times and places would be able not only to remember Christ's self-sacrifice and thank God for it, but they could actually—mysteriously—be present at it, and even enter into physical and spiritual communion with it by receiving the transformed bread and wine.

FLASHBACKS TO THE FUTURE

The filmmakers of *The Passion of The Christ* are Catholic Christians whose most important source of spiritual strength and renewal is participation in the sacrifice of the Mass. For them, as for all Catholics, every Mass breaks a hole through the wall of time and permits sinners to become truly present at Christ's incomparable act of love that redeemed sinful mankind from slavery to evil. By being there, and by receiving Holy Communion, it's as if they are really present with the Apostles at the Last Supper and with Christ at Calvary. They can unite themselves directly, fully to Christ. They can offer their lives in union with His to give honor to God, to repair for sins, and to receive His own strength to bolster their frail faith, hope, and love.

The flashbacks to the Last Supper highlight this vividly. Christ's hands are being nailed to the cross; in the flashback His gesturing hands provide a visual identification between the symbolic lamb and the real Lamb, Christ Himself. When the soldiers tear His tunic from His shoulders, the Last Supper scene captures Jesus pulling the cloth off the unleavened bread, which He is about to consecrate. When Jesus is hanging on the cross, the flashback reveals the moment He consecrates the wine into His own blood, blood that was "to be poured out for many for the forgiveness of sins." Immediately the film takes you back to Calvary where that very blood streams down His arms, drips from those same hands.

All through the flashbacks, Christ's actions are drawn from the perspective of the Apostle John, author of the fourth Gospel. This Gospel contains more explicit theological commentary than the other three. Throughout Christ's Passion, John seems to have been the least affected emotionally. Only in the flashbacks do you really see John's heart. He has not been sharing the suffering of Christ as viscerally as Mary and Magdalene. Instead, he has been in awe of it. He has been relating it in his mind to the many times Jesus had told His Apostles that He would have to undergo suffering. Over and over Jesus tried to get them to understand that He must offer Himself in sacrifice, so that, as He said at their last meal together, "the world may know that I love the Father, and as the Father hath given me commandments, so do I."[92] The film purposely emphasizes John's recognition of the meaning behind the sacrifice.

Making sure that the audience saw not only Christ's hideous death, but also the reason behind it—within the symbols of the Passover Seder—and the way to benefit from it—represented by the allusions to the

92 John 14:31.

Mass—was essential. Christians through the centuries have found hope by plugging in to Christ's own sacrifice, by being able to participate in the one sacred action that changed the course of history. Connecting to that extreme love during Mass is the warp and woof of the spiritual life for Catholic Christians. It's where the many "No"s they have selfishly said to God are mercifully swept away by Christ's perfect "Yes."

MAGDALENE'S MIRACLE

One of the unique moments during the crucifixion occurs when the soldiers have already nailed Christ to the cross and turn Him over to pound over the ends of the nails. There's a certain logic to it—the weight of Christ's body may have eventually pulled the nails loose from the free-standing cross. The idea didn't come from studying the history of crucifixion techniques. It came out of the writings of a seventeenth-century Spanish nun, Mary of Agreda.[93] She emphasized the presence and activity of angels throughout the life of Christ and Mary (and even in her own life). As she describes the crucifixion, she recounts that when the soldiers turned over the cross, angels prevented it from smashing Christ into the ground. Instead of ground there was, miraculously, empty space. (Essentially, Jesus was suspended in air.) This lessened the Savior's suffering.

Some viewers during the early screenings hardly noticed the detail, others were nonplussed, thinking it absurd that after Christ has suffered so much God would intervene supernaturally to relieve that particular pain. The film has something else in mind. Admittedly, the detail of turning the cross

---

[93] Her comprehensive, four-volume *Mystical City of God* narrates the life of Christ from Mary's perspective. It differs considerably from Blessed Anne Catherine Emmerich's meditations, in that Mary of Agreda adds a plethora of theological and spiritual reflections, commentary, and interpretation. Unlike Sister Emmerich's book, Mary of Agreda's book has caused considerable controversy among theologians and non-theologians alike.

over, from a dramatic standpoint, makes a gut-wrenching impression, but the little miracle goes beyond merely saving Christ from excruciating pain. It is another gesture of Christ's love, another instance of Him bolstering a soul's teetering faith in the midst of His deadly combat.

Mary of Agreda mentioned nothing about the miracle being seen by any of the bystanders, but the film shows it as being witnessed by Magdalene. From the moment Magdalene, Mary, and John arrive at Calvary, Magdalene begins to break down emotionally. Her wailing and weeping grows into inconsolable grief. She is losing hope, her faith is wavering, her soul is as frayed as Christ's body. But even so, she stays with her Lord. Her love prevails, and she won't leave, she won't abandon her Savior.

When Magdalene sees the soldiers turn the cross over, her total breakdown seems imminent. She collapses on the ground and can scarcely look up. But her love can't keep her eyes away, and that love is rewarded. She looks at her battered Lord and sees the miraculous suspension of the Cross. Her weeping ceases. She can barely believe what she is seeing. She glances around—no one else sees it (except the audience who see through her eyes, share her experience). She begins to straighten up; her face is filled with new determination, with new strength.

The miracle wasn't for Christ, it wasn't for the sake of lessening His pain; it was for her. Her pain was too much to bear; His love was too deep to abandon her. Through the miracle, He reminded her that He was suffering freely, that He was still the Lord, that this was not outside God's plan. It was enough. Magdalene's faith and hope return, shoring up her exhausted love. For the rest of the film she stands strong. She still suffers, but now she suffers with hope.

No one else inside the movie sees Magdalene's miracle, but the audi-

143

ence does. On Calvary Christ performed it for her sake, but the filmmakers included each viewer in Magdalene's situation. Just as Christ knew that she needed something, needed to see something to provide relief from the horror, so the audience needs some visual relief.

The sequence also carries theological weight; the audience learns more about Christ from the miracle, just as Magdalene does. The little miracle is really Jesus' gift to her at that moment. He is thinking about her, not about Himself. She has peace amid the anguish. She sees the miracle and thinks, *This is amazing; He's not touching the ground; that doesn't happen. There's something a lot bigger going on here. It wasn't just my imagination; He wasn't kidding! He really is divine!* At that point she regains her composure, emerging from her sorrow into serenity. Magdalene has hope, and so does the audience.

MARY'S "AMEN"

Mary, on the other hand, gets no miracle. Her suffering is raw. It's deeper than Magdalene's. A mother's love goes deeper, but so do her faith and her trust. Mary is able to hang on to her hope, even as God asks her to make her own ultimate sacrifice: to surrender her own son to total destruction.

Maia Morgenstern, who played Mary, discovered a gesture that brilliantly expresses this spiritual triumph. The intensity of her performance, her expressions, and her postures, are almost enough to convey her inner struggle and victory. But while they were filming the crucifixion sequence, she found a way to bring it into focus. As Christ is lifted up on the cross, she stands up with Him, clutching two handfuls of gravel and dirt, as if just barely hanging on to her hope. Once the cross falls into place and Christ's doom is assured, you see her anguish give way to strong and tender acceptance and solidarity. The camera cuts to her hands, and her clenched fingers relax, the sharp stones and broken earth spill to the ground. She has given up her son, echoing His own surrender to the Father's will.

Mary symbolically adds her Yes to Jesus' "Thy will be done." At the end of the crucifixion sequence that symbol becomes a word. Just as she had prayed "So be it" when her son's Passion began, after He has uttered His last words she prays it again: "Amen." It doesn't appear in the Bible or in the film's subtitles, but it fits. It seems as though she had to say that, she had to find closure for her experience, as if ending a prayer. That's how Jews and Christians end their prayers: "Amen.... So be it." This whole experience has been a living prayer for Mary, an offering of herself, her son, and her love. She needed to say "Amen."

Clutching the rocks was Maia's idea. No one told her to do it; she instinctively came up with it on her own. Maia was constantly experimenting to find the right way to play each moment. She describes the gamut of emotions she went through to find the right combination for Mary, whom Christians have venerated for two thousand years: "She [Mary] went through everything: anger, resentment, despair, vengeance, and everything in between. But in the end it was just a matter of a mother's love for her son. She couldn't do anything else. What else could she do? She had to suffer with Him."

CHAPTER 9

━ ┼ ━

CHRIST'S FINAL WORDS

· SPOTLIGHTING FORGIVENESS

Christ talks more during the crucifixion than He does at any other time in the film. The flashbacks include His longest lines (except those in Gethsemane), and from the cross He speaks what Christian tradition has long referred to as "The Seven Last Words." These statements are found in the New Testament, and each one is considered a seminal testimony to the meaning of Christ's Passion. As the film portrays, it would not have been easy for Jesus to speak at all under those circumstances, so each phrase mattered. The film makes sure to include all seven, not adding or subtracting.

Well, there was one addition. According to the Gospel accounts, all the Seven Words seem to have been uttered from Jesus on the cross, but the film has Jesus speaking the first one—Father, forgive them, for they know not what they do"—while they're still nailing Him to the cross. He can't get the whole line out, because He is writhing in such pain (and because Jim was having difficulty with last minute script changes that day), but He can still say more than once, "They don't know.... They don't know...." Why is He shown saying this line before the cross was elevated? The obvious answer is that Christ would have been saying that phrase the whole time, during the whole length of the Passion. The entire point of the sacrifice is so that sins can be forgiven.

The same line, the full version, also appears when Jesus is dying on the cross. Caiaphas challenges Him to show some kind of sign that He really is the Messiah, and then walks off in righteous disgust that someone so pitiful could claim to be the Promised One of God. As he walks away, Jesus again says the first of the Seven Words, "Father, forgive them, for they know not what they do."

Why include that line twice? It's important to realize that God's forgiveness is being enacted at the very moment when they're torturing and condemning Him. That's what the Passion is all about; it's the revelation of God's love, which in turn is the source of Christian faith and hope. Forgiveness ties it all together. By featuring the line twice, the film depicts two different kinds of forgiveness. While being nailed to the cross, Jesus forgives those who are responsible for His physical torment. When He's hanging from the cross He forgives those guilty of moral violence, those who are rejecting His person and message, who are publicly humiliating Him. Jesus greatly suffered the consequences of both genres of sin; it was necessary to show both dimensions of His forgiveness.

When Caiaphas hears Jesus' response, he "stops dead in his tracks. He slowly turns, looks at Jesus with amazement," as the screenplay elaborates. It's a critical moment—the first time anything Jesus has said or done has penetrated Caiaphas' heart or even made any kind of impression on him at all. It is a glimmer of hope for Caiaphas, sparked by a word of forgiveness.

Dismas, the thief hanging on Jesus' left, notices the exchange and is moved to start a dialogue that will lead to the second of the Seven Words.

He says to Caiaphas, as if in rebuke, "Listen … He prays for you." It's a sign of Dismas' moral awakening. This criminal has been watching Jesus the whole time, drinking in His every look and gesture. The love exhibited by Christ's self-sacrifice has penetrated this thief's heart in a way that it hasn't yet penetrated Caiaphas' (who for the first time in the film is left speechless), or Gesmas' (the other thief). Dismas responds to the love he has witnessed by making an act of faith, reaching out to Jesus with a prayer of humble hope: "Lord, remember me when thou shalt come into thy kingdom." Jesus grants his prayer: "Amen, I say to thee. This day thou shalt be with me in paradise." (Only these two lines—the prayer and the response—are recorded in the Gospels, the rest of the dialogue is interpolation, though based on scriptural allusions.[94])

Everyone in Jerusalem during those days had heard of Jesus and what He had been doing; Dismas was certainly no exception. He too knew that Christ had entered the city less than a week before amid acclamations of praise and exaltation. But it wasn't such abstract knowledge that was able to renew his heart; seeing Jesus hanging on the cross, forgiving the very enemies who had mutilated Him beyond recognition, and even praying for them— that's what converted him. That was the kind of Savior he could relate to, the kind of God he could pray to. A Christ like that inspires hope.

THE HUNGRY CROW

The tentative emergence of goodness and hope is interrupted by the rude cackle of Gesmas, who, unlike Dismas, simply can't see anything special about this Galilean weakling. As his malice boils, a crow perches on his cross.

94 See Luke 23:42-43. The screenplay's addition of lines at this point makes Jesus' response to Dismas' prayer even more fitting. Dismas' comment to Caiaphas can be understood as a public declaration of his adherence to Christ. In that light Jesus' response becomes the fulfillment of a promise: Every one therefore that shall confess me before men, I will also confess him before my Father who is in heaven (Matthew 10:32).

(In Christian iconography, crows symbolizes death and sometimes damnation.) The crow pecks out Gesmas' eye.

Was that added scene too "Hollywood" as some viewers thought? Not necessarily. The idea came from the documented research of real crucifixion. The criminals would hang there, dying, for days. Birds would rip their rotting putrid flesh even before they were dead; swarms of flies would infest their wounds. That's what crucifixion was like. The film couldn't show an entire five days of agony, but it needed to communicate that aspect of the horror.

The event also bears a spiritual significance. From the first time you see Gesmas, you detect something diabolical about him. It's as if a Devil has entered into him and is tormenting him from the inside. The appearance of the crow is not something simplistic, like a punishment. The Devil was operating through this man, attracting horrible things to him. The viewer sees the encounter unfolding cinematically and can't help being drawn in to it, as horrible as it is.

This artistic interpretation also works well theologically, since the "punishment" for sins in the Christian tradition of spirituality is neither random nor generic. Sin is a purposeful deviation from the wonderful, wise plan of the Creator. The goal of that plan is human happiness, on earth for a little while and then forever in heaven. Therefore, the natural consequence of deviating from that plan is missing the goal, missing out on happiness, or on some aspect of it. If you are greedy or slothful or lustful, for instance, the result will be suffering associated with greed, slothfulness, or lust; the consequence naturally fits the crime. Gesmas closed his heart and mind to Christ, refusing to see the love Jesus' Passion revealed. The crow pecks out his eye as a symbol of the spiritual blindness that was his undoing.

"I THIRST"

As life ebbs out of the crucified Jesus, Mary and John come closer to the cross, drawn by His love to accompany Him more intimately during His last moments. When they approach He forces out the third of the Seven Words, "I thirst." The Gospels record that the guards overheard Him and held up a sponge soaked in cheap wine (or vinegar) on the end of a hyssop stick to Jesus' lips.[95] That little drink of vinegar also fulfilled an Old Testament prophecy.[96]

The Gospels record that Christ's crucifixion began around noon, and His dead body was taken down three or four hours later. The last time He would have drunk anything would have been at the Last Supper. Considering His overwhelming blood loss from the beatings and flagellation, and the physical exhaustion of the forced march with the cross to Calvary under the hot sun, Jesus' thirst must have been severe.

But thirst is an odd type of suffering. It is physical, but hidden. As Jesus hangs on the cross, His torn flesh rubbing against the rough grain of the wooden cross, His head and brow pierced with thorns, His hands and feet throbbing from the nails, it seems curious that Jesus doesn't complain about any of those excruciating pains. Instead, He mentions only being thirsty. In one sense, nothing could be done to alleviate the monumental pain at that point, whereas Jesus could still take a drink to relieve His parched throat. Christian tradition has always seen another meaning included in those words, however. Just as Jesus called to mind the suffering of physical

95 The film used the spear instead of a hyssop stick (as recorded in St. John's Gospel account), following another detail from Anne Catherine Emmerich's meditations. St. John's mention of the hyssop stick calls to mind once again the relationship between the New and the Old Covenants, because hyssop sticks were used to sprinkle the sacrificial blood on the altar in the Jewish Temple.

96 And they gave me gall for my food, and in my thirst they gave me vinegar to drink (Psalm 68:22).

thirst, Christians believe He was simultaneously bringing to light another hidden suffering—that of spiritual thirst, the thirst of unrequited love.

God didn't *have* to send a Savior to fallen humanity. And yet He did, Christians believe. Why? Out of love. In the early chapters of his Gospel, St. John summarizes the entire message of Christianity in one simple but amazing phrase: "For God so loved the world as to give his only begotten Son, that whosoever believeth in him may not perish but may have life everlasting."[97] God wants to save sinners; He wants to welcome them back into His friendship by forgiving their sins and renewing the trust in their hearts. He thirsts to give them back authentic meaning and unquenchable hope. When Jesus gasps, "I thirst," it points to more than His burning desire for a drink; it reveals the even more ardent desire for hearts, for the reciprocal love of those He loves so deeply.

THE MOTHER'S HOUR

At that point, Mary can no longer watch only in silence. She speaks her heart, reminding Jesus of the deep union between them by calling Him "flesh of my flesh, bone of my bone, heart of my heart." It is more than mere poetry, since she truly is His mother. Then she explains with wonderful conciseness the depth of her suffering as she stands by helplessly watching her son die: "My son, let me die with you." He has been the entire meaning of her life, naturally and supernaturally. Without Him to care for and to follow, she will have nothing left to live for; with Him suffering so horribly, she cannot bear suffering any less.

These words are not recorded in Scripture (according to the biblical account, Mary doesn't speak at all at the foot of the cross). The screenplay

97 John 3:16.

adds her words to help explain the meaning of the words Christ speaks in response. He looks into her eyes (again, Jim Caviezel is almost miraculously able to exude consummate spiritual strength in the midst of absolute physical debility), and then looks at John, the lone representative of his inner circle of disciples, and gives Mary a job to do: "Woman, behold your son." Looking at John, He further explains, "Son, [the word *son* is not pronounced at that point in the Gospel account], behold your mother." It is the moment when Mary, who brought Jesus into the world and is now with Him as He leaves the world, is given to be the spiritual mother of all the Christian faithful. Jesus will not let her die with Him, because she has more work to do, her mission isn't over. She will have to mother the infant Christian Church once Christ has returned to His Father, just as she mothered Christ Himself when He first came from the Father.

At the beginning of the sequence, Mary's weight of suffering seems to increase, almost anticipating the mission she is to receive. She staggers forward toward the cross, leaning against it and kissing Jesus' feet. Her lips redden with His blood. Like each of us, Mary must renew her hope at the fountain of lasting spiritual strength—the inexhaustible love of Christ, symbolized by His blood, and made tangible in the bottomless suffering of His Passion.

FINISHING THE JOB

Christ's final three phrases reflect intimately what is going on in His mind and heart as His sacrifice nears its climax. Most of the spectators have returned to the city, and the atmosphere of loneliness is accented by Gesmas' harsh taunt to Jesus, "They are running away, abandoning you. You are alone. There is no one left. No one." The words echo the temptor's words Jesus heard at the start of the Passion, in the Garden of Gethsemane, suggesting a final attack on His trust in the Father, now that His suffering has reached its fullness. Jesus' response seems at first to be, indeed, a final break in His confidence. He lifts his head and cries in desperation, "My God, my God, why have you forsaken me?"

How can He have gone through so much up to this point and kept His faith, and now suddenly rebel against His Father, question His Father's love? He didn't. The Gospels record this prayer, which seems at first glance to be a cry of rebellion and despair. In fact, however, it is a line from the Psalms; it activates the meaning of its context, the meaning of the psalm as a whole. By pronouncing the first verse of Psalm 21, Jesus is engaging the entire psalm to express the prayer of His heart at that moment. As He hangs dying on the cross, rebuilding the bridge of trust between mankind and God that original sin had destroyed, the psalm shows that Christ's faith was not breaking as He cried aloud. Instead, His faith was taking its last triumphant lap through His path of blood and humiliation. Although His suffering was extreme, His love was more extreme, just as in the text of the psalm.

Psalm 21 summarizes the reason behind Christ's Passion and the fruits it will bear for the salvation of sinners in a new, everlasting Kingdom. Christians have always considered it one of the most eloquent prophecies of Christ's Passion. It was written by King David around the year 1000 B.C. Although it's long, it is well worth reading, as it provides a jarring glimpse into the Messiah's heart as He hangs on the cross about to die:

> *O God my God, look upon me: why hast thou forsaken me?*
> *Far from my salvation are the words of my sins.*
> *O my God, I shall cry by day, and thou wilt not hear:*
> *and by night, and it shall not be reputed as folly in me.*
> *But thou dwellest in the holy place, the praise of Israel.*
> *In thee have our fathers hoped: they have hoped,*

and thou hast delivered them.

They cried to thee, and they were saved:

they trusted in thee, and were not confounded.

But I am a worm, and no man:

the reproach of men, and the outcast of the people.

All they that saw me have laughed me to scorn:

they have spoken with the lips, and wagged the head.

He hoped in the Lord, let him deliver him:

let him save him, seeing he delighteth in him.

For thou art he that hast drawn me out of the womb:

my hope from the breasts of my mother.

I was cast upon thee from the womb.

From my mother's womb thou art my God.

Depart not from me.

For tribulation is very near: for there is none to help me.

Many calves have surrounded me:

fat bulls have besieged me, have opened their mouths against me,

as a lion ravening and roaring.

I am poured out like water; and all my bones are scattered.

My heart is become like wax melting in the midst of my bowels.

My strength is dried up like a potsherd,

and my tongue hath cleaved to my jaws:

and thou hast brought me down into the dust of death.

For many dogs have encompassed me:

the council of the malignant hath besieged me.

They have dug my hands and feet.

They have numbered all my bones.

And they have looked and stared upon me.

They parted my garments amongst them;

and upon my vesture they cast lots.

But thou, O Lord, remove not thy help to a distance from me;
look towards my defense.

Deliver, O God, my soul from the sword:
my only one from the hand of the dog.

Save me from the lion's mouth;
and my lowness from the horns of the unicorns.

I will declare thy name to my brethren:
in the midst of the church will I praise thee.

Ye that fear the Lord, praise him:
all ye the seed of Jacob, glorify him.

Let all the seed of Israel fear him:
because he hath not slighted nor despised
the supplication of the poor man.

Neither hath he turned away his face from me:
and when I cried to him he heard me.

With thee is my praise in a great church:
I will pay my vows in the sight of them that fear him.

The poor shall eat and shall be filled:
and they shall praise the Lord that seek him:
their hearts shall live for ever and ever.

All the ends of the earth shall remember,
and shall be converted to the Lord:

And all the kindreds of the Gentiles shall adore in his sight.

For the kingdom is the Lord's;
and he shall have dominion over the nations.

All the fat ones of the earth have eaten and have adored:
all they that go down to the earth shall fall before him.

And to him my soul shall live: and my seed shall serve him.
There shall be declared to the Lord a generation to come:
*   and the heavens shall shew forth his justice to a people that shall be*
*   born, which the Lord hath made.*

Having fulfilled all the prophecies, having drained the chalice of suffering to its last bitter dregs, and having parried the Devil's final thrust with a glorious flourish of trust, Christ knows He has finished His work. Catching His mother's eyes, as if to include her in His triumph, He pronounces the final report on His earthly mission of salvation, the mission foretold from the dawn of history and prepared for since the Fall: "It is accomplished." In the midst of His suffering, as it draws to a close, He is at peace, because He knows that it was part of the Father's plan.

His dying words, the simple expression of a filial trust that is the source of His peace—"Father, into Your hands I commit My spirit"—have strengthened and comforted countless Christians on their own deathbeds, words rising heavenward on their last breaths as well. Because Christ could be at peace in the midst of atrocious suffering, those who follow Him can find peace in the midst of their suffering; His enduring love spawns our unending hope.

CHAPTER 10

— ✠ —

DEATH

THE COSMIC BATTLE RETURNS

The Gospels speak of extraordinary natural phenomena accompanying Christ's self-sacrifice on the cross. As His death draws near, the sky darkens and the sun is eclipsed. When He breathes His last, an earthquake opens tombs and tears in two the sacred curtain of the Temple's inner chamber (symbolizing the end of the Old Covenant, or rather its fulfillment in Christ); the dead rise and are seen walking the streets of Jerusalem.[98] It wasn't hard to include most of these cosmic signs in the film, in fact, it was a lot easier than was originally planned.

The cast and crew were still down in Matera, and running behind schedule. Looking ahead to the Calvary shots that still had to be filmed, they were facing, it seemed, at least another week of shooting. Then the weather started to change. It looks like special effects, but it wasn't; an unbelievable weather pattern suddenly appeared, and it fit perfectly with what they still had to film. The dark sky, the sun, the wind—the whole combination. As the

98 See The Gospel of Matthew, chapter 27.

weather changed they would set up and shoot whatever scene fit that particular climate. It happened again and again. Instead of taking a week, they wrapped the Calvary sequence two days later.

During the storm that rolled in on these last Calvary shots a young assistant director, Jan Michelini, was standing up on the hill holding an umbrella over the grip while the storm was coming in. Thunder was rumbling and lightning was flashing, so they called cut and told everyone to take cover. All of a sudden a huge lightning bolt hit Jan's umbrella. It went right through his hand and his whole body. The umbrella was charred and Jan was standing there in the rain, stunned, his fingertips blackened. But nothing happened to him. Other than a swollen hand, he was fine. He just stood there smiling.

This was no normal lightning strike, though; it had a second chapter. The same assistant director was hit by lightning again, almost a year later, when they were back in Rome dubbing. They had decided to add the Sermon on the Mount flashback. Italy hadn't had any rain all summer. (In fact, people were dying all over Europe because of the drought and the tragic heat wave.) They lugged their equipment to the outskirts of Rome and started shooting. A few hours into it producer Steve McEveety got a call from the city reporting that a storm was on its way in. He could hardly believe it, because of the summer drought, but when he spotted the thunderheads rolling in, they rushed to finish.

Jim Caviezel was standing on the hilltop preaching to the crowd, and Jan Michelini was with him. By this point everyone could see the storm approaching. As soon as the first drops started to fall they called cut and they were packing it in. Right then, a bolt of lightning came out of nowhere and hit Jan, holding an umbrella, exactly as before. Producer Steve McEveety was close by and saw the lightning hit Jan, and he also saw some sparks jump over and hit Jim. For an instant Jim actually looked like he had lightning coming out of his ear. Once again, no one was seriously hurt. Moments like that were adding flavor to an already spicy project.

Weather conditions helped the filmmakers get the footage they needed for the violent natural phenomena accompanying the crucifixion. But they had to engineer the earthquake themselves, with camera techniques and some special effects. The earthquake, explicitly mentioned in the Bible, was too important a detail to exclude. It's considered the turning point of history, the moment when everything starts over; it even knocks the tough Roman soldiers out of their comfort zones. In fact, the film follows Christian tradition by showing two of the soldiers, Abenader and Cassius (later known as St. Longinus) react by believing in Christ's Messianic identity. (Scripture recounts only one of the soldiers at Calvary making an act of faith.)

If they included the earthquake, why not also include the dead people coming back to life and wandering around the streets of Jerusalem, a biblical detail that emphasizes the efficacy of Christ's sacrifice and the salvation it achieved? They had to make an artistic judgment on that one. They thought a lot about it. It's biblical, and theologically it's important, but how do you make it work cinematically? To show that is to risk making the last scenes border on scenes from a horror movie. Mixing in such an image could easily have been distracting or ambiguous.

GOD'S TEAR

The film adds a significant detail to emphasize the meaning of these extraordinary natural phenomena. When Christ's heart slows, laboring more and more haltingly, then finally stops, the camera cuts to a high aerial view of Calvary. Simultaneously, all sound disappears. The screenplay's directive is particularly eloquent at this point: "Everything becomes, ever so briefly, still and silent. Nature, in shock, turns inside-out. Sound is sucked out of the air, as if it were offensive. Motion becomes stillness, paralysis. Light is extinguished and becomes darkness. Silence of death."

But the screenplay stops there. Only later did they decide to add one more final effect. The aerial point of view dissolves into a drop of water that cascades slowly down onto the hill of Calvary, passing in front of the crucified Jesus, and crashing into the stony ground below. With that crash, the earthquake begins; the aftershocks stun the soldiers, Caiaphas, and his cohort, Pilate, the bystanders. It's more than a special effect; it's God's tear. His Son just died. Sin killed Him. It matters to God. The tear, an incarnation of God's mercy, shatters the old fallen order and initiates the new creation. It's the profile of love in a sinful world: mercy, forgiveness, compassion. It topples the old kingdom of selfishness and sin and becomes the foundation of the new Kingdom, the one that will last forever.

THE SAVING FLOOD

The storm and the earthquake jolt the bystanders back into action. The Gospels explain that the leaders of the Sanhedrin had asked Pilate to remove the dead bodies from the crosses out of respect for the Passover celebration that was beginning that evening. With that in mind, the soldiers break the legs of the thieves to expedite their suffocation. When they come to Jesus the soldiers see He is already dead, so they only pierce Him with a spear to make doubly sure. The film shows more complex motives for these actions. The guard who goes to break Jesus' legs is reluctant to do so, his faith having already been kindled. When he catches Mary's eye, he knows that he can no longer treat Jesus—even a dead Jesus—like an ordinary criminal. His act of faith is rewarded. When he pierces Christ's side, water and blood gush out in miraculous quantities, as if to confirm his new, frail faith.

Only the Gospel of John records this detail of water and blood coming out Christ's pierced side. Medical doctors interpret it as an indication that the spear reached Jesus' heart, where what was left of His blood had disintegrated into its component parts—a sign that the cause of death was neither loss of blood nor suffocation, but a broken heart. The way the film portrays the incident the amount of fluids pouring out of the corpse is shocking. It should be shocking. It's another miracle, in fact, the one that finally converted Cassius (St. Longinus), so its supernatural quality is appropriate.

Christian spiritual writers and theologians have always seen the water and blood as symbols of the sacraments of the Church, most especially of baptism and the Eucharist (the name given to the bread and wine that have been consecrated during Mass). This underscores the New Creation theme so evident throughout the film. Through the sacraments, the signs of communion with Christ, men and women enter into the New Covenant and become members of the new Chosen People, the Church.

The water and blood motif recalls biblical Old Covenant details that prefigured baptism and the Eucharist—the Red Sea, for example (water that looked red in color), through which the People of God in the Old Covenant passed as they were being freed from slavery in Egypt. Even the waters of Noah's Flood (which would have been mixed with the blood of the many sinners who perished in it), symbolized a fresh start for the human race. The generous outpouring of blood and water seems to show, at least viscerally, life coming from death. It manifests the hope bred by Christ's unconquerable love, a love that gave everything He had for the forgiveness and salvation of His brothers and sisters, down to the last drop of His blood.

The Calvary sequence is completed with the last shot of Jesus being taken down from the cross, lying lifeless, in His mother's arms. She looks at Him with unspeakable sorrow and unquenchable love, and then she looks at the camera, at the audience. She breaks the "fourth wall" in that moment.

What is she saying with that look? Benedict Fitzgerald has no doubts. "She's saying, 'Don't forget. Don't forget. He did it for you.' And that is the real message of the film. It's a testimony to a truth that we can't, we simply cannot, forget. It's an act of un-forgetting. It's *alētheia* (a Greek word translated into English as *truth*, but its literal meaning is *un-forgetting)*."

The image of Mary holding her dead son's body at the foot of the cross is a familiar one in Christian art. It invariably calls to mind one of the world's most loved and renowned sculptures, Michelangelo's *Pietà*. The film's version is similar to Michelangelo's, but not exactly the same. For one thing, it includes other people, most notably John and Magdalene. Also, as the camera pans out, the wind continues to blow through the figures' hair and clothes, so that the tableau always remains cinematic, not static, never becoming a photograph or the imitation of a painting. Most important, however, is the difference in Mary's posture. Here's how one art historian describes it:

> The most compelling interplay between viewer and film occurs, however, during [the] representation of Michelangelo's *Pietà*. Mary holds her Son in the exact same manner, one hand cradling his body and the other hand open toward the viewer. The variation comes in that while Michelangelo's Mary gazes solemnly down at her son, [the film's] Mary looks straight out at us. The movie draws to a close provoking a full and conscious acknowledgment of whom this suffering has been for.[99]

99 "Ultimate Hero Movie: An Art Historian's View of *The Passion*," Elizabeth Lev; Zenit News Agency, www.zenit.org

CHAPTER 11

⊶ ✠ ⊷

RESURRECTION

Without the death of the victim, a religious sacrifice is incomplete; only total obliteration can signify one's total dependence on God's favor. In Christ's case, His death also expresses the extent of His love. He himself had defined total love during the Last Supper: "Greater love than this no man hath, that a man lay down his life for his friends."[100] The archetype of heroism is total self-sacrifice for the sake of the beloved. It is an act that says more eloquently than any other, "I am glad that you exist; I want you to exist, to be all that you are meant to be; I want it so much that I will even give up my own life to make it happen."

That is how one modern philosopher has defined the virtue of love, and that is what Christ's death on the cross says to every person created: "I am glad that you exist, I want you to exist, to have 'life, and have life more abundantly.'"[101] He wanted it so badly that He was willing to hand Himself over to the powers of evil, to pay the price for the redemption of sinners.

100 John 15:13.

101 This is how Jesus describes the goal of His earthly mission. See John 10:10.

If it had ended there, the world may have been impressed by Jesus' goodness. But someone who is good is not automatically worthy of one's faith or hope. The Resurrection, the real conclusion of Christ's sacrifice, adds a crucial element to His incomparable goodness: incomparable power. As He explained, "I have the power to lay my life down and to take it back up again."[102] The Resurrection, as mysterious as it is, is Christ's identity card. If He had not risen from the dead, as the Old Covenant had predicted the Savior would,[103] He would not be a true Savior, because He would be weaker than the powers of darkness, which had introduced evil, suffering, and death into the world.

Since He did rise from the dead, He demonstrates that the powers of darkness have no power over Him. They gave it their very best shot, but His love is stronger. "Many waters cannot quench charity."[104] That kind of love, that unconquerably strong love, is the kind of love you can build (or rebuild) a life around. The film recognizes this. Some critics try to make light of Christ's sacrifice. They say the Romans killed four thousand Jews that year, and one more was no big deal. But from the Christian perspective it was the ultimate big deal. Countless people were crucified, but only one ever got back up again. Only one person came back to life and walked away. That does indeed make a big difference.

It was essential for the Resurrection to be part of the film. But how do you show something so extraordinary and make it look believable? One option was to show the resurrected Christ encountering one of His disciples or Apostles, as the Gospels record. But that would, in essence, be the start

---

102 John 10:18.

103 See for example Hosea 6:2; 2 Kings 20:5; Exodus 19:11; the Book of Jonah; et al.

104 Song of Solomon 8:7.

of a whole other story, the story of the Resurrection. This movie was about the Passion. Co-screenwriter Benedict Fitzgerald explains how they first stumbled across the idea they finally used.

"I was visiting Florence and took my children to the Academia [the museum that houses Michelangelo's famous statue of David]. Most people don't realize how many wonderful paintings there are in that museum. I was looking at some of them, and suddenly one caught my eye. It was a painting by Andrea del Verrocchio, Da Vinci's mentor. And it showed Christ's Resurrection—not His post-Resurrection appearances, but the Resurrection itself. It showed Him sitting on the empty tomb and looking at the wounds in His hands. It mesmerized me. And that's when I knew that we had to do the same thing; somehow we had to show the *Resurrection*, not the appearances, because the Resurrection really was the conclusion of the Passion."

And that's what they did. The rock rolls back of its own accord, letting in a stream of sunlight (that doesn't exactly accord with the Gospel accounts, which seem to indicate that the stone was rolled back later by an angel, but it works cinematically). The light rests on the white shroud just as the body of Christ is mysteriously freed from it. On the one hand it looks natural—you see only sunlight, linen, and rock. On the other hand it is entirely supernatural—the body simply leaves the shroud behind, passing through the linen fibers just as sunlight passes through a windowpane. Then the camera focuses on the resurrected Christ Himself.

His youth and strength have returned, and His face shows a fresh eagerness and joyful determination, as if He is about to go forth on a great task. You see none of His horrible wounds. The contrast to the last glimpse of His tortured and broken body is shocking—is it really Him, has the Passion really happened? Maybe it was only a dream. But as He steps forward to begin the next stage of His redeeming mission, His right hand comes into view. Yes, it is the same Christ—the hole that the spike made is visible. It appears glorious, not gruesome. His other wounds were erased, but not these. His pierced hands are telltale signs of His self-sacrificing love, of His unconditional willingness to forgive. His suffering has come to an end, but the story of His love and forgiveness has only just begun.

They decided not to extend the Resurrection sequence, even though the Gospels all end by narrating a series of encounters between the resurrected Christ and His Apostles and other disciples. For forty days Christ mingled with His followers, as the New Testament records, "To whom also he shewed himself alive after his Passion, by many proofs, for forty days appearing to them, and speaking of the kingdom of God."[105] Much Christian doctrine is derived from these encounters, but their lessons are complementary to the great lesson taught by the Passion. That was *the* lesson, the living lesson, that this film is really meant to tell.

105 Acts of the Apostles 1:3

CHAPTER 12

✛

WHAT ABOUT A SEQUEL?

Will there be a sequel? That was one of the most asked questions after the early screenings, one which never received a direct answer. The Passion is the ultimate hero story—the definitive act of self-sacrificing love. Nobody ever did more, nobody ever could. So if it's the ultimate hero story, and if great movies are great hero stories, wouldn't this mark the end of the line? Not necessarily. There are other hero stories that are still worth telling—stories about "love in the little things" type of heroism. Those stories could be told. The world needs to hear those stories too.

That's the kind of heroism that Christ's love has been inspiring ever since He gave His life on the cross two thousand years ago. He exemplified heroism bolstered by faith in the power of good to triumph over evil, nourished by hope in the love of God who would die to give every man, woman, and child life now and forever. It's the kind of heroism that the Apostle John, writing to the first Christian communities in his old age, identifies as the true mark of those who believe in Jesus:

In this we have known the charity of God, because he hath laid down

his life for us: and we ought to lay down our lives for the brethren....
My little children, let us not love in word nor in tongue, but in deed and
in truth. In this we know that we are of the truth and in his sight shall
persuade our hearts.[106]

106 1 John 3:14-19.

APPENDIX

BIOGRAPHY OF ANNE CATHERINE EMMERICH[107]

An Augustinian nun, stigmatic, and ecstatic, born September 8, 1774, at Flamsche, near Coesfeld, in the Diocese of Munster, Westphalia, Germany; died at Dulmen, February 9, 1824.

Her parents, both peasants, were very poor and pious. At twelve she was bound out to a farmer, and later was a seamstress for several years. Very delicate all the time, she was sent to study music, but finding the organist's family very poor she gave them the little she had saved to enter a convent, and actually waited on them as a servant for several years. Moreover, she was at times so pressed for something to eat that her mother brought her bread at intervals, parts of which went to her master's family.

In her twenty-eighth year (1802) she entered the Augustinian[108] convent at Agnetenberg, Dulmen. Here she was content to be regarded as the lowest in the house. Her zeal, however, disturbed the tepid sisters, who were puzzled and annoyed at her strange powers and her weak health, and notwithstanding her ecstasies in church, cell, or at work, treated her with some antipathy. Despite her excessive frailty, she discharged her duties cheerfully and faithfully. When Jerome Bonaparte closed the convent in 1812 she was compelled to find refuge in a poor widow's house. In 1813 she became bedridden. She foresaw the downfall of Napoleon twelve years in advance, and counseled in a mysterious way the successor of St. Peter. Even in her childhood the supernatural was so ordinary to her that in her innocent ignorance she thought all other children enjoyed the same favors that she did, i.e. to converse familiarly

107 From the online version of *The Catholic Encyclopedia* at www.NewAdvent.org. *The Catholic Encyclopedia*, Volume VI, copyright © 1909 by Robert Appleton Company. Online edition copyright © 2003 by K. Knight.

with the Child Jesus, etc.

She displayed a marvelous knowledge when the sick and poor came to the "bright little sister" seeking aid; she knew their diseases and prescribed remedies that did not fail. By nature she was quick and lively and easily moved to great sympathy by the sight of the sufferings of others. This feeling passed into her spiritual being with the result that she prayed and suffered much for the souls of Purgatory whom she often saw, and for the salvation of sinners whose miseries were known to her even when far away. Soon after she was confined to bed (1813) the stigmata came externally, even to the marks of the thorns. All this she unsuccessfully tried to conceal as she had concealed the crosses impressed upon her breast.

Then followed what she dreaded on account of its publicity, an episcopal commission to inquire into her life, and the reality of these wonderful signs. The examination was very strict, as the utmost care was necessary to furnish no pretext for ridicule and insult on the part of the enemies of the Church. The vicar-general, the famous Overberg, and three physicians conducted the investigation with scrupulous care and became convinced of the sanctity of the "pious Beguine," as she was called, and the genuineness of the stigmata. At the end of 1818 God granted her earnest prayer to be relieved of the stigmata, and the wounds in her hands and feet closed, but the others remained, and on Good Friday were all wont to reopen.

In 1819 the government sent a committee of investigation which discharged its commission most brutally. Sick unto death as she was, she was forcibly removed to a large room in another house and kept under the strictest surveillance day and night for three weeks, away from all her friends except her confessor. She was insulted, threatened, and even flattered, but in vain. The commission departed without finding anything suspicious, and remained silent until its president, taunted about his reticence, declared that there was fraud, to which the obvious reply was: In what respect? and why delay in publishing it?

About this time Klemens Brentano, the famous poet, was induced to visit her; to his great amazement she recognized him, and told him he had been pointed out to her as the man who was to enable her to fulfill God's command, namely, to write down for the good of innumerable souls the revelations made to her. He took down briefly in writing the main points, and, as she spoke the Westphalian dialect, he immediately rewrote them in ordinary German. He would read what he wrote to her, and change and efface until she gave her complete approval. Like so many others, he was won by her evident purity, her exceeding humility and patience under sufferings indescribable. With Overberg, Sailer of Ratisbon, Clement Augustus of Cologne, Stollberg, Louisa Hensel, etc., he reverenced her as a chosen bride of Christ. In 1833 appeared the first-fruits of Brentano's toil, "The Dolorous Passion of Our Lord Jesus Christ according to the Meditations of Anne Catherine Emmerich" (Sulzbach). Brentano prepared for publication "The Life of The Blessed Virgin Mary," but this appeared at Munich only in 1852. From the manuscripts of Brentano Father Schmoeger published in three volumes "The Life of Our Lord" (Ratisbon, 1858-80), and in 1881 a large illustrated edition of the same. The latter also wrote her life in two volumes (Freiburg, 867-70, new edition, 1884).

[Sister Emmerich's] visions go into details, often slight, which give them a vividness that strongly holds the reader's interest as one graphic scene follows another in rapid succession as if visible to the physical eye. Other mystics are more concerned with ideas, she with events; others stop to meditate aloud and to guide the reader's thoughts, she lets the facts speak for themselves with the simplicity, brevity, and security of a Gospel narrative. Her treatment of that difficult subject, the twofold nature of Christ, is admirable. His humanity stands out clear and distinct, but through it shines always a gleam of the Divine. The rapid and silent spread of her works through Germany, France, Italy, and elsewhere speaks well for their merit. Strangely enough they produced no controversy. Dom Guéranger extols their merits in the highest terms (*Le Monde*, April 15, 1860).

Sister Emmerich lived during one of the saddest and least glorious periods of the Church's history, when revolution triumphed, impiety flourished, and several of the fairest provinces of its domain were overrun by infidels and cast into such ruinous condition that the Faith seemed about to be completely extinguished. Her mission in part seems to have been by her prayers and sufferings to aid in restoring Church discipline, especially in Westphalia, and at the same time to strengthen at least the little ones of the flock in their belief. Besides all this she saved many souls and recalled to the Christian world that the supernatural is around about it to a degree sometimes forgotten. A rumor that the body was stolen caused her grave to be opened six weeks after her death. The body was found fresh, without any sign of corruption. In 1892 the process of her beatification was introduced by the Bishop of Münster.

BIOGRAPHY OF FATHER PETER GALLWEY
AUTHOR OF **THE WATCHES OF THE PASSION** [108]

Born at Killarney, November 13, 1820; died in London, September 23, 1906; one of the best-known London priests of his time. He was educated at Stonyhurst, joined the Society of Jesus at Hodder, September 7, 1836, was ordained priest in 1852, and professed of four vows in 1854. As prefect of studies at Stonyhurst (1855-1857), he made important improvements in the method of study. In 1857 he was sent to the Jesuit church in London, where—except for an interval of eight years during which he held the provincialate and other offices—he spent the rest of his life.

He was a man of deep spirituality, much venerated as a preacher, spiritual director, and giver of retreats; he was also noted for his love of the poor and his earnest advocacy of almsdeeds. So great were his energy and enterprise that he set his stamp on all he undertook. Several London convents and Catholic institutions owe largely to his zeal and encouragement both their first foundation and their successful subsequent development. His writings comprise among others: "Salvage from the Wreck," sermons preached at the funerals of some notable Catholics (1890); "The Watches of the Passion," (1894), a series of meditations on the Passion, embodying the substance of his retreats; a number of sermons, tracts, and other small publications, mostly of a topical kind.

---

108 "Augustinian" refers to the religious community that Sister Emmerich belonged to before it was disbanded by the government. An Augustinian community of nuns (or monks—both male and female communities are still in existence) lives as a religious family, praying and working together according to a rule of life that allows them to dedicate every minute of their existence to praising God and interceding for the salvation of souls. The Augustinian rule traces its origins back to St. Augustine of Hippo (author of *The Confessions* and *The City of God*, among other works), who died in the year 430.

DEFINITION OF "STIGMATA"[109]

Phenomenon in which a person bears all or some of the wounds of Christ in his or her own body, i.e., on the feet, hands, side, and brow. The wounds appear spontaneously, from no external source, and periodically there is a flow of fresh blood. The best known stigmatic was St. Francis of Assisi. During an ecstasy on Mount Alvernia on September 17, 1224, he saw a seraph offer him an image of Jesus crucified and imprint upon him the sacred stigmata. Blood used to flow from these wounds until the time of his death two years later. He tried to conceal the phenomenon but not very successfully. Since that time scholarly research has established some three hundred twenty cases of stigmatization, among them more than sixty persons who have been canonized.

Authentic stigmatization occurs only among people favored with ecstasy and is preceded and attended by keen physical and moral sufferings that thus make the subject conformable to the suffering Christ. The absence of suffering would cast serious doubt on the validity of the stigmata, whose assumed purpose is to symbolize union with Christ crucified and participation in His Passion.

Through centuries of canonical processes, the Church has established certain criteria for determining genuine stigmata. Thus the wounds are localized in the very spots where Christ received the five wounds, which does not occur if the bloody sweat is produced by hysteria or hypnotism. Generally the wounds bleed afresh and the pains recur on the days or during the seasons associated with the Savior's Passion, such as Fridays or feast days of Our

109 From the online version of *The Catholic Encyclopedia* at www.NewAdvent.org. *The Catholic Encyclopedia*, Volume VI, copyright © 1909 by Robert Appleton Company. Online edition copyright © 2003 by K. Knight.

Lord. The wounds do not become festered and the blood flowing from them is pure, whereas the slightest natural lesion in some other part of the body develops an infection. Moreover, the wounds do not yield to the usual medical treatment and may remain for as long as thirty to forty years. The wounds bleed freely and produce a veritable hemorrhage; and this takes place not only at the beginning but again and again. Also the extent of the hemorrhage is phenomenal; the stigmata lie on the surface, removed from the great blood vessels, yet the blood literally streams from them. Finally true stigmata are not found except in persons who practice the most heroic virtues and possess a special love of the Cross.

FOR FURTHER READING

The Gospels of Matthew, Mark, Luke, and John, in the *Holy Bible*

The Watches of the Passion, by Peter Gallwey

The Passion and Death of Our Lord Jesus Christ, by St. Alphonsus de Ligouri

The Passion and Death of Our Lord Jesus Christ, by Archbishop Alban Goodier

The Life of Christ, by Fulton J. Sheen